STORES

OF THE YEAR

No. 13

STORES

OF THE YEAR

No. 13

Martin M. Pegler

VISUAL REFERENCE PUBLICATIONS, New York, NY

Copyright © 2001 by Visual Reference Publications, Inc.

Visual Reference Publications, Inc.
302 Fifth Avenue
New York, NY 10001

Distributors to the trade in the United States and Canada
Watson-Guptill Publishers
770 Broadway
New York, NY 10003

Distributors outside the United States and Canada
HarperCollins International
10 East 53rd Street
New York, NY 10022-5299

Library of Congress Cataloging in Publication Data:
Stores of the Year No. 13

Printed in China
ISBN 1-58471-057-8

Book Design: Judy Shepard

CONTENTS

INTRODUCTION

Imagine a retail store without mirrors, without salespersons, with hardly any actual merchandise to touch, to feel, to caress, to actually see the true color of and see how that color suits your complexion. Imagine a retail store that shows a single garment hung in front of a sweep of curved metal that is equipped with touch screen monitors and keyboards. Imagine a catalog store of almost a century ago that has been "modernized" and high-teched into the 21st century with all sorts of futuristic, technological, gadgets, gimmicks, overscaled graphics and computerized imagery and you have what some believe will be the store of the future. At a recent Globalshop in Chicago just such a concept store was unveiled.

The concept behind the design is something called "biometrics" which is the science of personal identification. The identification can be by means of fingerprints, iris scanning or facial recognition. To create this "Starwars" store, the shopper is photographed upon entering the store by means of cameras located at the entrance. When the "facial recognition" is made the shopper is greeted by name by an electronic voice. Just how personal can that be? Since there are no racks of garments to look through, tables loaded with clothes to pick through or shelves arranged by color or size to scan, the shopper communicates via a computer keyboard in front of the single representative garment to some Wizard of Oz hidden behind a screen or burrowed away in some attic. When the customer-to-be arrives at the dressing room the garment selected arrives via pneumatic tube. Imagine watching the garment you want to try on oozing out of a plastic tube? Entertaining—isn't it? Now—does the shopper look in the mirror? No mirror! An image of the "dressed" shopper is telecast on a plasma screen and by computer the shopper can relay this image to friends and family at home. AND—to make the shopping experience fast and easy—if somewhat impersonal, she can order the garment on the computer in the dressing room and it will be waiting for her as she leaves the store. All transactions and payments will be by "plastic." Is this REALLY what shoppers go out of their houses for and drive to malls or shopping streets for? For "bricks, clicks and tricks"?

Some retailers and designers are listening to the shoppers! We have collected some of these examples in book 13 of Stores of the Year. In a recent study of what shoppers consider "the ideal shopping experience" that was conducted by the Kelley School of Business of Indiana University, it was found that first and foremost they want "knowledgeable and courteous sales help." They don't want anything that intrudes on their "personal privacy." Dr. Raymond Burke of the E.W. Kelley School of Business said, "People want the basics in their shopping experience and they are only interested in technology to the extent that it makes shopping faster, easier and more economical." As in the stores shown in this volume, this is where the "future" lies in Retail store design. When the new technologies are integrated into a warm, inviting, human scaled, retail setting and the store offers shoppers choices, options, selections, service and ease of shopping, the store will succeed. We may want to go "high-tech" and we may want to take advantage of all the technological advances but there will always be shoppers who want to see, touch, feel, and "taste" products. "Bricks and clicks"—without the "tricks" can work when they assist the shopper and afford him/her an appeal to all the senses—not a "virtual experience"—but a real one.

Our selections have been gathered literally from around the world: England, Scotland, France, Italy, Germany, Spain, Denmark, Japan, Chile, Brazil, Mexico, Canada and across the U.S. The trends are all here: the "Casual-ing of Fashion." The more relaxed, the more easy going, dress-down fashions are growing more and more important and even the "minimalist" boutiques are "easing" up. Stores are warm, rich, welcoming and comfortable. They are humanized—they are residentialized—they are for relaxing and for enjoying. More often than not we are finding men's and women's fashions together in a single specialty store whether the store sells high fashions, designer clothes, sportswear or jeans. We have included several vendor shops as they appear in major department stores because that trend is also growing. And everywhere we can see the "entertainment factor" integrated into the total shopping experience.

Can you imagine the day when instead of sitting down to a romantic dinner with candlelight, flowers and bubbling champagne we stand at the water cooler and "dine" on pills, pressed packages of non-definable but nutritious blends that contain all the virtues and values of real food-except the TASTE? You can't imagine that? Then you aren't ready for the Store of the Future and "shopping" with Capt. Kirk in some cold, sterile, space-ship of a store.

Martin M. Pegler

STORES

OF THE YEAR

No. 13

POLO RALPH LAUREN

W. Palm Beach, FL

DESIGN: **Backen Arrigoni Ross,** San Francisco, CA
PRINCIPAL: **Richard Beard**
ARCHITECT: **Shawn Sasse**
SR. V.P.: **Michael Gilmore**
PROJECT ADMINISTRATOR: **Laura Brezel**

For Polo Ralph Lauren
VP OF STORE DEVELOPMENT: **John Heist**
PROJECT MANAGER: **Michelle Kirschstein**

WORTH AVE., in Palm Beach, FL, is the address of boutiques of many noted designers. A series of landmarked buildings stand as testimonials to the gracious, grand and fabulous days of the late '20s and '30s when those with money could flaunt it in this wealthy enclave. The repetitive motif of arches, columns and the rhythmic arcades fill the street and now Polo Ralph Lauren has taken up residence in one of those historic structures. In a space of 14,500 sq. ft.—on two levels—men's, women's and home furnishings are presented with elegance and style. Exterior loggia entries provide a traditional way of entering the new store and the rear courtyard was restored and opened to the store space turning the store into what could easily have been a Palm Beach mansion of the 1920's.

The interior has been completely

redesigned to blend the well established Polo image with the lush style that distinguished the residences of that period. Backen Arrigoni Ross, of San Francisco, who are the designers/architects of most of the recent Polo Ralph Lauren stores, also designed this one. The main retail spaces are divided into main, grand rooms—each with ancillary side rooms and alcoves "knit together by classic galleries and loggia spaces." An interior arcade runs around the main level. It supports a mezzanine sales area and it also creates a soaring central atrium. Centered in the atrium is an eight sided wood unit that anchors the space and atop it is an exuberant display of greenery in assorted pots. The woodwork, throughout, is the dark, rich signature mahogany color which contrasts with the cool white of the walls, ceilings and arches. Cast coral stone was carefully detailed to recreate one of Palm Beach's loveliest historic materials: coral stone. The coffered ceilings and the inner surfaces of the arches are richly ornamented with anaglypta. Most of the floors are dark stained wood overlaid with natural

sisal carpets or oriental style rugs. Rattan and woven wicker seating is provided in the men's area while on the mezzanine, in individual salon-like settings, white upholstered sofas and chairs in front of French mantels and fireplaces suggest elegant withdrawing rooms. Crystal chandeliers add to the illusion. Connecting the two levels is an elegant black wrought iron and white marble staircase that angles up. The walls in the stairwell as in the small "boutiques" are lined with paintings while in the Men's area there is a profusion of antique prints, artifacts and such. Antiques, ginger jars, vases, urns, toss pillows and other accent pieces pick up the blue color that is used throughout to highlight the otherwise neutral setting.

In addition to the atmospheric light of the chandeliers and table lamps, the interiors of the wood "armoires" are self illuminated, and recessed spots provide the overall ambient and accent lighting.

MARK SHALE

Michigan Ave., Chicago, IL

DESIGN: **Charles Sparks + Associates,** Westchester, IL
PRINCIPAL IN CHARGE: **Charles Sparks**
PROJECT MANAGER: **Stan Weisbrod**
LIGHTING DESIGNER: **Don Stone**
COLOR/MATERIALS: **Fred Wiedenbeck**
DOCUMENTS: **Jim Meseke**

ARCHITECT: **Kurtz & Associates,** Des Plaines, IL
IN-HOUSE DESIGN TEAM: **Steve & Scott Baskin**
PHOTOGRAPHY: **Michael Roberts,** Chicago, IL

I N A DARING MOVE, Mark Shale—an upscale men's and women's apparel shop—left its former home in a four story building and moved its "new look" into a new location across the street on Michigan Ave. in Chicago. The "simpler" and more modern Mark Shale now occupies the third and fourth floors of an enclosed mall and uses the 20,000 sq. ft. to showcase the changes in the clothing industry. Steve Baskin, co-president of the Mark Shale stores, said, "Clothes have changed and have become more casual and less formal. We felt that the store should reflect that."

Starting with a concept that evolved from the Kansas City store that he had previously designed for Mark Shale, Charles Sparks of Charles Sparks + Associates created this design that is "a simpler, cleaner design" than the earlier ones. The new space still maintains that wonderful feeling of spaciousness. "It has a series of spaces that act like rooms, without the four walls." To define the different areas in the linear floor plan, the designers used high, open, wardrobe-type fixtures/dividers and brightly colored geometric area rugs. The ceiling architecture and lighting plan overlay a uniform pattern on the loose fixture plan thus allowing for lighting any grouping or rearrangement of fixtures or "rooms."

The Women's area has been given more prominence with a generous display in the windows facing the mall's traffic aisle and the curved, sweeping fixtures and walls that naturally leads the shoppers through the space. The emphatic and dramatic chocolate brown, laminate-covered oval columns that make strong linear statements on the floor also serve as display niches for featured garments. The cash wrap counters are actually large "hospitality desks"; stone tops on stainless steel legs. According to the designers they "are contoured for comfort, ease and customer interaction."

Smaller workstations are located throughout where shopper and salesperson can relate in a one-on-one situation when making selections. All the fixtures were designed to be "thin, light and elegantly detailed." They combine brushed stainless steel and wood with ribbed glass.

The Men's area is more linear in feeling and here the inspiration for the store design is more apparent. "The store was inspired by the luxurious simplicity and functionality found in the work of the early modernists of the '20s and '30s." Adding to this look is the combination of the elegant fixtures, the expanses of light colored, natural wood and the bold colors that appear as geometric insets in the otherwise neutral beige carpeting. The vibrant red wall adds dramatic impact to the curved wall of the

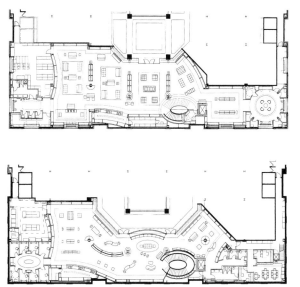

oval staircase that connects the two levels of the store. The fixtures and millwork are planar, simple and "carefully proportioned to create spaces void of ornament."

To satisfy the requirements of their upscale shoppers, special attention was paid to the design, arrangement and space devoted to the dressing rooms. "We wanted the dressing rooms to be more inviting," said Charles Sparks. "With more walk around space it allows sales associates to work more freely with the customer." After researching the matter, the designers found that while men prefer a more centralized space where they can change and then work with a fitter/tailor, women prefer enclosed dressing rooms. Near the dressing rooms there is a water bar, comfortable sitting chairs and a variety of reading material for those who wait.

The mall-facing shop front features large areas of glazing which makes it possible for shoppers to see into a wide expanse of the store That, combined with the display of women's garments, allows the women in the mall to feel more comfortable about entering into Mark Shale. "Not only did they (Mark Shale) retain their old customers, they added new ones."

CORTEFIEL

Madrid, Spain

DESIGN: **Point Design, Inc.,** New York, NY
PRINCIPAL IN CHARGE: **Diego Garay**
PROJECT DESIGNER: **Ayumi Date / Luis Bruno**
COLORS & MATERIALS: **Howard Pasternack**
CLIENT TEAM: **Caroline Vlerick / Paula Aza**

CORTEFIEL, a chain of 80 outlets, needed to update its image to be competitive with the large number of retailers who have arrived on the scene in Spain in the last 30 years. Changing demographics also meant that the store's merchandise and design needed to appeal to a younger clientele—the 25-40 year old men and women.

Point Design Inc. of New York was called upon to create the design magic that would assist in the company's transformation. The challenge to the architects/designers was to "render a more hip store" that would not alienate or offend the existing customer base while—at the same time—"create a balanced interior that showcases both men's and women's clothing elegantly." "In essence, the chal-

lenge of the redesign was to create a dramatically different atmosphere without making radical changes."

In a two level, 10,000 sq. ft. space, the prototype was rolled out. The upper level features the private labels and the collections while the ready-to-wear and casual-wear are on the lower level. The designers used a light colored palette with dark brown woods and black accents. The "boxy" store design has many sharp, clean lines and throughout the store the accent lighting serves to lead the shopper's eye to the garments on display. Two light colored travertine marbles were used on the floors to distinguish the departments. Near the entrance, a touch of color was introduced with the hand laid mosaic tiles which stand out from the cool, subdued palette of the rest of the

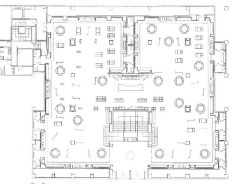

Floor Plan

space. The fixturing systems are constructed of light and dark woods, stainless steel and glass.

In one area men's and women's shoes, bags and gloves are presented in a cool, almost white, space. The stainless steel display tables and benches are accented with black lacquer trays and black leather upholstery. Shoes and

bags are displayed on black lacquer shelves against illuminated frosted glass panels. The cash desk also plays a strong black on white pattern in the space it is situated in nearby. White, open back frames showcase the handbags on the black wall behind the cash/wrap.

The open well in the center of the main level is surrounded by a glass and stainless steel railing. The stairway leads down to the lower level. Throughout the store couches, chairs and benches are provided and black shaded lamps add a "residential" feeling to selected seating areas.

This redesign has already been introduced into 20 of Cortefiel's Madrid stores and the remaining 60 are scheduled to be transformed within the next two years.

MAGASIN

Kolding, Denmark

DESIGN: **Jorn Hanser S.A.,** Kolding, Denmark

MAGASIN is a chain of specialty department stores located throughout Denmark. The new store that opened in Kolding was designed and fitted with fixtures by Jorn Hansen, S.A.

The design firm followed through on the smallest details to make this a prototype design that could be carried into the next century. The resulting space is light and spacious and furnished in brushed stainless steel, light colored maple wood and sand blasted glass.

The merchandise is presented in individual and distinctive "worlds": men's, women's, children's and home fashions. By doing this the store is bright, easy to shop and the merchandise is comfortably arranged for the shoppers perusal. Magasin is also capitalizing on the open selling trend in the perfume area where the personal selection selling is proving very successful.

"With a view to creating a display of articles which is as up to date and inspiring as possible, the seven worlds (in the store) have not been divided into shops but appear as well laid out units—all in the same modern and simple design." The Jorn Hansen firm, long distinguished as designers and manufacturers of floor and wall systems, have created several systems that are used throughout to keep the merchandising flexible and adaptable to changing seasons and/or needs. They also help to keep a consistent look throughout.

GRAND GALLERY

Kiev, Ukraine

DESIGN: **Umdasch Shop Concept,** Amstetten, Austria

PROBABLY the most fashionable address in Kiev, the capitol of Ukraine, is Grand Gallery. The 1,500 square meter store, newly enlarged, redecorated and refitted by Umdasch Shop Concepts, is filled with small vendor boutiques that wear such noted names as Diesel, Escada, Sport, Matinique, and Mc Gregor. Larger shops are devoted to merchandising Lagerfeld and Steinmann.

Situated in the center of the city on Hreschatik Blvd. in a handsome old building, the designers had to update and upscale the overall setting without losing any of the gracious, elegant detailing of the original. Some of the areas have twenty foot high ceilings and the walls, ceilings and columns are enriched with decorative stuccowork (anaglypta). "We had to very carefully fit our systems into this fine gallery."

To update and complement the period salon-like setting, the designers used Umdasch's fittings and fixtures that would blend—and almost disappear—in the setting. They used their

Classic system for the wall installations and in other areas they installed the Para system and integrated it in stage-like sections. The light colored floor tiles, the off white walls and ceilings and the tall columns all add to the open and spacious feeling of Grand Gallery. Uplights, on the columns, pick out the decorative, dimensional stuccowork on the ceiling and the light is then reflected back on to the merchandise hung on the Para panels attached to the four sides of the columns. On the upper level, the floors are covered with a cool, gray green carpet or finished in natural wood. Here, the marble columns carry the Para panels. Track lighting is combined with ceiling attached halogen lights to illuminate the space

and the merchandise. The two levels of the store are connected by a pair of grand marble staircases—to either side of the entrance. They are enriched with marble balustrades.

The men's areas, on both levels, are distinguished by the natural wood floors and the light wood fixtures. The height of the main level allowed the Umdasch designers to create a "deko-stage" above the wall systems for the display of merchandise. The display stage is located opposite the staircases and directly in front of the entrance foyer.

KENNETH COLE

Grant Ave., San Francisco, CA

DESIGN: **In House Store Design Team**
CREATIVE DIRECTOR: **Kenneth Cole**
SR. STORE DESIGNER: **Montgomery Rush**
DIR. OF STORE DESIGN & DEVELOPMENT: **Christine Russo**
ARCHITECT: **Sat Garg, Akar Studio,** Santa Monica, CA.

THE KENNETH COLE name has long been associated with a prestigious line of shoes and bags for men and women. Recently, however, the designer has added apparel lines to complement the leather lines. The Kenneth Cole retail settings personify the life-style trend in store design and retailing. Christine Russo, Director of Store Design and Montgomery Rush, Sr. Store designer, working under the creative direction of Kenneth Cole create unique, one-of-a-kind, eclectic and simply wonderful living spaces where the assorted product lines are shown together. Ms. Russo says that they "do not have the feel of a store. Rather they are comfortable living room settings where people can spend time and hang-out around the product." Illustrated here is the new San Francisco store where, on three levels, the multi-faceted Kenneth Cole's apparel and shoes are shown.

The actual retail settings are cool, light and neutral. The walls are either exposed brick or concrete-plaster that has been artfully troweled by imported artisans. The entrance level floor is paved with Egyptian stone and a contemporary black metal staircase connects the three selling levels. Menswear is prevalent on the main level. Here sportswear, outerwear, shoes and briefcases are set out on dark stained wood counters and in the perimeter wall units with display shelves above and cabinet space below. "I" beams serve as fascia trim over the wall units while other metal construction beams and girders make vertical statements on the floor. The

front end of the store soars while a mezzanine set over the rear end of the floor creates an intimate space for the showing and trying on of the shoes.

The mezzanine houses an optical shop with an in-house optician. There is also a display of men's sportswear on this level. The second level looks like a living room setting with an eclectic mix of period pieces set out on the stained, custom wood floors overlaid with area defining rugs. The semi-sheer white curtains on the windows and the floor and table lamps add to the casual, relaxed,

at-home feeling which Ms. Russo talked about.

The third floor is devoted to men's tailored clothes, dress shirts, ties and fashion accessories. Here, the open wall cabinets of dark stained wood are complimented by the white interiors and shelves inside these perimeter units. The visual merchandising combines face out with shoulder out plus neatly stacked folded garments. Black upholstered chairs of another era add a relaxed feeling to the otherwise black, white and wood setting.

Throughout, the lighting is per-

fection. The light plan varies from level to level and in each area the plan combines recessed incandescent with hidden washers, floor lamps and—on the main level—chandeliers. TV monitors are judiciously placed in the retail setting: they are there but they don't intrude into the generally casual, easy-going ambiance. The construction motif reoccurs throughout: the beams, the girders, the exposed brick, the concrete plastered walls, the black metal railing that reappears on each floor. Accenting the no-color, no-time or period settings are giant black and white photo murals and simply-framed photographs. Here the merchandise stands out and the shopper fits in.

DERIMOD

Nisantasi, Istanbul, Turkey

DESIGN: **Zoom Tasarim Proje Uygulama,** Istanbul, Turkey
INTERIOR DESIGN: **Atilla Kuzu**
ARCHITECTS: **Levent Cirpici & Bulend Ozden**

DERIMOD has established itself in Turkey as one of that country's leading designers/manufacturers of leather goods. A great part of the firm's output is exported to Europe and Asia. In an effort to establish a firmer market in Turkey and among the many tourists who come to Istanbul looking for fine leatherwear, Derimod commissioned the Istanbul-based design firm, Zoom Tasarim Proje Uygulama, to create a prototype for a retail store. In this chain of stores the company plans to present its American and European styled products to locals and tourists.

Nisantasi is "a pleasant region in Istanbul where most fashion trends of the world take place." Since the store is located in this upscale, fashion-forward area, the designer, Atilla Kuzu, attempted to "create a perfect harmony between the products and the interior of the store." In order to accomplish this, the setting is neutral: light, clean and open and in no way does it detract from the product presentation.

The openness of the space is furthered by the use of glass shelving—a "transparent material"—and the shelf and hanging

systems are supported by an aluminum mast system. The wall fittings are recessed in illuminated niches. "By this system, the products are presented as individual illuminated themes." To enhance the open look the walls and floor are white and the material palette has been limited to glass, aluminum and wood. The sloped ceiling panels provide the indirect light source for highlighting the product display while also serving as reflective surfaces.

"Derimod gives a high quality effect to its customers by the interior design of the space as well as the products being presented."

BOETIEK 32

Breda, Holland

DESIGN: **Kamp Design Associates,** Amsterdam, Holland
INTERIOR DESIGN: **Kees van Schoten**
VISUAL MERCHANDISING: **Chantal van Manen**
FITTINGS: **Harmeling Interieur,** Rijssen, Holland

BOETIEK 32 is a 27-store chain of moderately priced fashions for 18 to 35 year old men and women who really care about what's in fashion. The stores are divided into lifestyle areas: city and work, casual and jeans.

A signature feature of the Boetiek 32 store is the light cove that traverses the store and not only creates two ceiling levels but it also carries lighting for the selling floor. In contrast to the gridded wood ceiling is the rough, natural pine planking that is laid on the floor. "This gives the store a feeling of elegance and rusticity at the same time" and bridges the lifestyle themes from the dressed-up city clothes to the casual wear and jeans for fun and relaxing.

Though the design calls for large, rectangular, multi-level wood tables on the floor in the casual area and standing rectangular wood frames in the women's suit area, all fixtures are acces-

sible, easy to reach and to merchandise. The hardware on the free-standing fixtures and on the wall units are interchangeable. The cash/wrap desk "looks somewhat like a bar" and it has a flexible back wall that can be used for stock and display. All the fittings "were especially designed for a coordinated presentation" and thus clothes can be hung and/or shelved as desired. The open backed wall units are set in front of the white walls and all the units are constructed of a reddish brown wood that is trimmed with a blond wood for the "elegant/ casual" effect.

The modularization continues even to the curtained-off changing rooms. Each season a new accent color is introduced on a focal wall, a column or in an area to indicate a change and "to accentuate the mood of the clothes for that season."

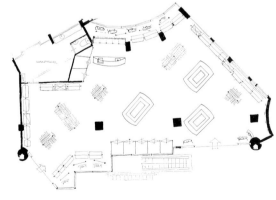

KAREN MILLEN

Brompton Rd., London, U.K.

DESIGN: **Brinkworth,** London, U.K.
DESIGNERS: **Adam Brinkworth & Silka Gebhardt**
PHOTOGRAPHY: **Richard Davies**

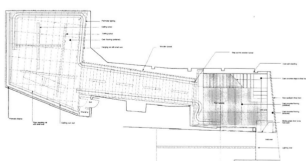

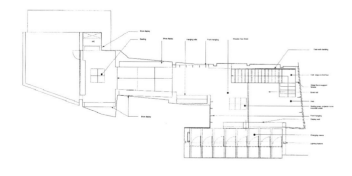

KAREN MILLEN'S fashions are well known in the U.K. and there are presently over 50 retail outlets for her clothes. For the past decade Brinkworth, a London-based design firm, has worked closely in evolving individualistic, "risk taking design concepts" for the unique stores. The new and quite radical—yet simple and elegant—flagship store is located on Brompton Road in Knightsbridge near Harrod's and Harvey Nichols.

The boldest design statement is the two story glass facade which is now the tallest shop window in Knightsbridge. The etched glass effect is accomplished by the use of white vinyl film over the glass. According to the designer, Adam Brinkworth, "The vinyl is not permanent, so Karen Millen could simply remove it or it could be changed to bring in different colors including patterns and maintain a fresh look." At night the window is a "film projection screen" while during the day silhouetted shoppers can be seen moving about. Especially commissioned films—some from a local film school—are projected as entertainment out on the street.

The entrance to the shop is in an alleyway on the far side of the store. This was necessary to achieve the "white out" facade. A bright strip of colored light hangs over the entrance in the alley. "The colors gently changes, complementing the projections." By placing the entrance on the left

and the staircase, to the upper level on the far right, the designer opened up the entrance area to an impressive double height space. To increase the open volume, the mezzanine was cut back. The shopper is drawn into the back of the shop through a narrow "tunnel" where the floor, walls and ceiling are sheathed in dark wood. Beyond is a dramatic wall that "changes the backdrop of the clothes." This is a prismatic display unit such as is used in outdoor, billboard advertising. Over this Brinkworth has applied three laminates to the prisms: metallic, white and black.

The dark wood of the "tunnel" reappears on the staircase that is cantilevered out from the gray terrazzo wall. The mezzanine mirrors the main floor and this time the shopper is lead through a gray glass corridor to where the shoes are displayed. Brinkworth has indeed created a new conceptual approach for this flagship store "with beautiful detailing and a clever use of space."

REINALDO LOURENCO

Sao Paulo, Brazil

DESIGN: **Studio Casas,** Sao Paulo, Brazil
Arthur de Mattos Casas

LOOKING TO UPDATE a relatively new store and get into more of a feeling of the future, the noted Brazilian fashion designer, Reinaldo Lourenco, called upon Arthur de Mattos Casas, the architect/designer, to create the totally new, minimalist look.

The architect used simple, native materials to accomplish this new feeling. "I used common and simple materials such as cement and plaster—but in a special way," says Sr. Casas. With the plaster he was able to "curve" walls so that the bi-level space is filled with voluptuous, sweeping arcs that envelop the shopper and the few garments on view. By "reburning," a special finishing process, Casas was able to affect a stone-like appearance on the concrete poured floors. The space is white and light with the natural daylight introduced and the towering ceilings of the 990 sq. ft. ground level. Together they "create the theatrical and dramatic mood for the space." For the young, affluent shoppers who are tuned in to "the fashion world movement" and have the purchasing power necessary to buy Lourenco's designs, this dramatic and theatrical setting seems to be perfect.

Ambient light streams down from the light fixtures way up on the ceiling while

the garments, shown face-out at eye
level, are illuminated by lights hidden
behind and beneath the sweeping fascias.
Adding to the light and the illusion are
the floor-to-ceiling mirrors that not only
echo the arcs of the walls but also, in the
dressing room area, replay the yards of
falling white drapery that cover the individual changing rooms. The soft drapery
also adds relief from the smooth wall
surfaces.

The 430 sq. ft. mezzanine is reached
via a well lit, all-white staircase. The rail-
ing-less, narrow stairway is secured by a
glass wall that also borders the narrow
passageway. Upstairs, in smaller, more
intimate spaces, special customers are
given extra-deluxe attention.

Adding occasional color accents—like
a bright yellow cash/wrap desk—punctu-
ates and enlivens the space without
detracting from the product display.

LAURA II

Fairview Mall, North York, ON, Canada

DESIGN: **Burdifilek**
DESIGN DIRECTOR: **Diego Burdi**
MANAGING PARTNER: **Frank Filek**
DESIGNER: **Lester Agnew-Kata**
PHOTOGRAPHY: **Ben Rahn, Metropoli Pictures,** New York, NY

"THE LAURA woman is a conscious career woman who demands good quality and value. She is successful and reflects this in the way she dresses. She is a contemporary woman who values femininity and elegance."

Burdifilek, architects and designers, have created several Laura stores in Canada. The stores stock sportswear, formal dresses and outerwear as well as jewelry and accessories. Thirty five designer and private labels are housed in spaces that range from 4,000 to 6,000 sq. ft. Finishes and materials are carefully selected to complement the everchanging product and to give the space "a rich and

timeless elegance." In all of the Laura divisions (Laura, Laura Petites, Laura ll) a pastel palette is used and ash veneers are applied to the fixtures. Signature materials such as porcelain tile flooring, brushed nickel, sandblasted glass fixtures, custom lacquer finishes and inset area carpets appear in all.

The finishes at Laura ll are the lightest with pale gray, taupe, ecru and a soft blue/green as the palette for the

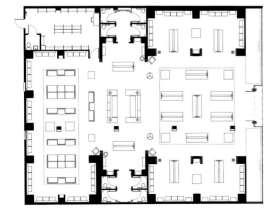

lacquered finishes and wall paints. The ash veneer is finished in a light, semi-matte taupe wash which is complemented by the natural beige porcelain tiles on the floor. Adding warmth, texture and some sophistication is the gray/taupe looped carpet.

The store is compartmentalized into departments to emphasize "the range of categories and to ease stress in the shopping experience." A floor and wall hanging system was created that gives total flexibility to product presentation and also allows the retailer to "create merchandise stories" To create mood and focus, there is custom lighting and a variety of illumination levels. The fitting rooms are luxurious with custom wallpapers and rich fabrics used for seating and the draperies in the closing partitions. "This softens the look of the area and allows easier communication between clerk and customer."

BRAEMAR

Oakville Place, Toronto, ON, Canada

DESIGN: **Hirschberg Design Associates,** Toronto, ON
PHOTOGRAPHY: **Richard Johnson**, Interior Images

BRAEMAR is a well established and highly respected chain of Women's clothing stores in Canada with many satisfied return customers. With the Oakville Place store, designed by the Hirschberg Design Group of Toronto, Braemar's broke away from its familiar image to meet new innovative objectives regarding merchandise and format development. The objective was to accomplish this new prototype design without alienating the long time clientele.

One of the most startling changes was going from a 5000 sq. ft. space to a 2500 sq. ft. space in order to lower construction, fixturing and lighting costs. Still, the designers had to integrate all the special elements that Braemar customers have come to expect without sacrificing quality. A new exterior sign program highlights merchandise in the window while drawing the shopper into the store. The new, light scale fixtures give the interior space a more residential ambience and that is further enhanced by the merchandise presentation. Combining two color programs, customers can now distinguish between the two clothing lines: Braemar Regulars and Braemar Petits.

Warm off-white walls and ceilings are combined with a soft, warm neutral carpet to open up the space and make it

seem more spacious. The floor and wall fixtures are constructed of a light, natural wood accented with white laminated tops. The walls are used for merchandise presentations and displays and the simple slotted system is adaptable and easy to change as needed. The lighting plan combines hanging pendant fixtures with recessed fluorescents and warm spotlights throughout to accentuate the wall displayed products as well as the on-floor displays.

The renovation of Braemar Oakville Place "responds to consumer driven needs and attitudes" and the results of the new look have surpassed expectations by the staff and been approved by the customers.

CORI

Iguatemi Shipping Center, Sao Paulo, Brazil

DESIGN: **Grid 3 International, Inc.,** New York, NY
PRESIDENT: **Ruth Mellergaard**
PLANNING & DESIGN: **Marcelo Albertal**
JOB CAPTAIN: **Errol Demagajes**

For Cori
V.P. OF MERCHANDISING: **Renato Pasmanik**
V.P. OPERATIONS & MARKETING: **Carlos Magno**

To SET THE STAGE for the line of women's wear and also attract shoppers in the Iguatemi S/C, Grid 3 International created an open facade of big windows framed in marble for the Cori store. The raised platform in the windows brings the mannequins into prominence while the angled storefront minimizes the glare of the lights in the mall.

Inside the store a light, neutral and minimalist palette of ipe (a local hardwood), brushed stainless steel and a warm white paint creates an "elegant contemporary setting" that emphasizes the clothing color, style and fashion image. In order to make the store easy to shop and at the same time help the customers to organize and coordinate their selec-

tions, the garments are arranged in wall closets and on tables. Visual clutter is avoided. Just as Cori clothes are utterly simple, the Grid 3 designers created a setting that reflects that "spare simplicity." For each Cori store the tables, closets, cash wraps and cappuccino bars are custom designed and built.

Cori hosts fashion shows which are taped and then played on prominently located video monitors located around the store. The brushed stainless steel cappuccino bar doesn't take up much space but it does play an active part in the store's everyday life. The cash wrap with its gently rolled ends is also finished with the stainless steel. In keeping with the store's image, the dressing rooms are

spacious and simple, yet fully equipped with all the niceties the customer might want. A stylish sitting area is provided with comfortable upholstered arm chairs for those who wait while others shop.

Throughout, black and white photography appears on the off-white walls framed in either black or natural wood. The floors are a combination of white washed and resined wood teamed with tiles of creamy travertine. To ensure good color rendition of the merchandise and also energy efficient lighting, the designers have specified color temperature matched tungsten halogen and fluorescent lamps along with some metal halides to create the pleasing lighting plan. In the dressing rooms the lighting not only enhances the clothing but the shopper as well.

STREET ONE

Hamburg, Germany

DESIGN: **Corsie Naysmith Int'l Design Consultants,** London, UK
FIXTURES/FITTINGS: **Vitrashop GmbH**, Weil Am Rhein, Germany

THE PROTOTYPE design for the new Street One retail shop was designed by Corsie Naysmith of London. Located in Hamburg, the German based retailer wanted a retail store that would appeal to 20-35 year old fashion aware, fashion conscious and value-smart shoppers. "Concentrating on the demands of today's customers, the shop offers up-to-the-minute commercial fashion with frequent new collections. With over 400 sites across Europe, Street One wanted a new more 'with-it' image and thus this new design," Stuart Naysmith, the design director of the project, said. "One of the unique aspects of Street One is the fact that they present twelve collections a year. We had to design a system that was

not only flexible but also provided rigidity in terms of display to ensure a consistent look throughout the stores." Another challenge was to design a look for the retail environment that would appeal to and reflect the lifestyle of the target market—in several different countries—and also be economical and adaptable to roll out across Europe.

The fixtures and fittings, manufactured and custom tailored by Vitrashop, are for three types of stores: flagship, High Street and shop-within-shop or Vendor shops. The solution is

"a clean, fresh environment with fashionable material components and an extremely adaptable shopfitting system that offers Street One a controlled flexibility with their merchandising." Vitrashop's "Stripe" system is very adaptable and does allow greater merchandising flexibility and more corporate control on the configuration of the shop fittings. "With such a vast roll out system," says Naysmith, "it is important to reduce the shopfit system to the minimum number of components in order to maximize profitability of each store."

The new interior, as shown here, is 140 sq. meters and the Hamburg operation features four components: glass-green laminate in accessories, silver wall panels for merchandising and display, bamboo flooring to emphasize lightness and "return to nature" and, as an accent, the red color taken from the Street One logo and signature identity. Together this palette creates an appealing and stress free environment for the shopper; a bal-

anced lifestyle setting. Balancing the rational features (the fixtures, fittings and the merchandise) are the emotional ones. Here it is the warmth of the lighting, the natural look of the wood fittings and floors, and the use of red on the columns, the seating units and the carpet in the 'corners of rest." Altogether the setting creates "an ideal synergy of features for a rational female customer who has the emotional need to feel totally at ease in the atmosphere where she buys her favorite brand."

The success of the prototype has resulted in a rapid investment and building program which means that all the Street One shops should be refitted within the next two years. The company also plans to further expand its vendor shop program with more shops-within-the-shop across Europe.

ELLE

Bluewater Mall, Outside of London, UK

DESIGN: **Four IV,** London
DIRECTOR: **Gregor Jackson**
SENIOR DESIGNER: **Michelle Barker**

THE SPRINGBOARD for the ELLE retail store was the fashion magazine of the same name and thus the concept was to make the shop "a three dimensional magazine." "The design challenge was to develop a 'kit of parts' that could be transferred world wide and would incorporate the various requirements of each country." "The diversity of the world-wide market required there be an attitude that with the smallest material or proportional change the design would allow the scheme to appeal to a different age group or give the brand the required variation in profile. The prototype store, shown here, was opened in the Bluewater Mall.

In keeping with the magazine theme, the shop front serves as the "magazine cover" with changing text headliners and strapliners floating in the window—"advertising the features" to the shoppers. The changing window displays become the "advertisements." Within the store, the seamless resin floor "becomes the glossy pages of the magazine" and the material palette and the lighting enhance "the feminine tonal variations" of the floating panels, furniture, walls and ceiling which all play with "the colours of make-up." This links back to the strong emphasis on beauty and beauty products in the magazine. The lighting in the store is bright and reflects off the white background. The merchandise is broken down into "stories" of product both on the perimeter and mid-floor fixture/fitting units.

The corporate red color appears on a curved wall and on the ellipse that appears with its own red shadow on the floor. The ellipse creates a feature zone. This is "the heart of the store and one of the pivotal brand statements." Promotions and special offers are presented here. The cash/wrap also serves as a reception desk: service is "the face" of the magazine. In addition, a large acrylic magazine wall emphasizes the international presence of the brand and the current magazine covers from around the world are on display here. Also, the availability of the magazine within the shop "allows the brand to be positioned within current global trends."

ODEON

Hamburg, Germany

DESIGN & SHOP FITTINGS: **Trend Store,**
a division of Barthelmess GmbH, Nurnberg, Germany
OWNER: **Johann C. Anthon/Matthias Lemcke/Wolfgang Krogmann**

IN A SMALL SPACE of 80 sq. meters the designers of Trend Store created a new look for the Odeon store. Odeon specializes in ladies' fashions and men's knitwear. To best show off the collection, Trend Store developed a system of oak veneers, stained high grade steel and glass.

The overall look of the shop is light, clean and symmetrical. Sitting on the white, epoxy-resined wood floor are the stylish, simple and functional floor fixtures/fittings which are made of a warm stained oak and glass. The walls and ceiling are tinted a creamy, vanilla white. The recessed wall cabinets and shelves—the same warm white—are illuminated with built-in, low voltage spot lights. Creating a dramatic and arresting effect is the focal wall panel of red with the store's name emblazoned across it in silver. This panel, on the rear wall, holds the design together. A giant photo blow-up of a woman in

red adds a second strong color accent to the space. To break the symmetry, the merchandise presentations on the two side walls are different.

Men's knitwear is located up front and a partial wall that serves as a background for the window display serves as the vehicle in which the menswear is hung. The partition is light enough and open enough not to close in the feeling of the store.

The fine materials and their refined applications add to the image of the upscale merchandise in the shop. Spots, recessed in the ceiling, provide the ambient light while the built-in, low voltage lamps complement the color of the garments on display.

VIVAVIDA

Sao Paulo, Brazil

DESIGN: **Ronaldo Saaraiva**

JUST AS fashions change and the shoppers' tastes and interests will change, the owners of the very upscale, fashion forward VivaVida company in Brazil continually changes the physical settings of their stores to keep up with the new and different trends happening all around. Their newest incarnation is the VivaVida store located in Sao Paulo's "noble district"—Higienopolis. According to Nardi Davidsohn, the director of the company, "Our new concept to retail is not only to continue to produce high quality clothing, but to inform and cater to our clients' needs with new information on fashion,

trends, fabrics and affecting a purchase adequate to one's taste and physical form."

Ronaldo Saaraiva was the architect/designer. He had to realize this retail concept: "The journey through senses, vision, touch, audio and accent" and combine new technologies with fashion and bring about a setting that is "harmonious and also balances the shopper's pleasures with her needs."

The collection was visually segmented. There is a "Sport" section with practical garments designed to satisfy the athletic customer. The "Weekend" grouping has casual and relaxing styles while "Basic" is for the career-oriented woman. For glamorous and special occasions there is the "Collection." In addition, professionally trained fashion consultants are there to guide and assist the clients in purchasing the right items for themselves as well as orienting them in the latest fashion trends.

To keep the clients aware of what is new and what is available to them, there are computer monitors that present all segments of the season's collection and a large TV wall covered with TV monitors. A 35mm short, especially produced in Rio de Janiero, entertains customers with a viewing of the latest books. Large photo blow-ups are used throughout to enhance lifestyle settings.

Throughout, the architect/designer and VivaVida worked to appeal to all of their clients' senses. Specially selected scents produced from oils and spices were introduced into the air conditioning system. The scent is "intended to arouse the senses and give a sense of comfort and well being." Bio-Music was added: music selected to stimulate the senses and emotions. "The exact location of each item in the store plays an important role in creating a positive and well balanced energy." The all-neutral off-white, beige and light natural wood setting provides a warm and relaxing setting where the client's well being is top priority.

MELANIE LYNE

Le Carrefour Laval, Quebec, Canada

DESIGN: **Burdifilek,** Toronto, Ont.
DESIGN DIRECTOR: **Diego Burdi**
MANAGING PARTNER: **Paul Filek**
DESIGNER: **Lester Agnew - Kata**
PHOTOGRAPHY: **Ben Rahn, Metropoli Pictures,** NYC

"THE MELANIE LYNE customer is confident and reflects this in her personal style and fashion choices. Image is very important to this customer as is looking current, well put together and refined." Melanie Lyne is the high-end concept store of the Laura's Shoppe's Women's retail store operation.

For the designers, Burdifliek of Toronto, the challenge was to create a flexible design since all 30 designer and private labels had to be showcased in this refined, 5400 sq. ft. environment. Melanie Lyne properties usually range from 4000 to 6000 sq. ft. and thus the design had to be adaptable to different size and shaped spaces. "The design language had to reflect the sophisticated confidence of the Melanie Lyne woman, define a strong identity in the marketplace and speak a higher price point than any and all of the other Laura concepts."

The design firm evolved a compartmentalized floor plan that would be easy to shop. It "positions the retail environment as well defined and respectful of

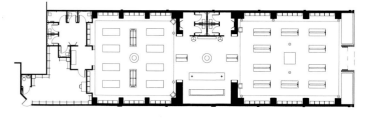

customer's 'needs' at the same time it gives the retailer the desired flexibility. "The merchandise is grouped by designer on adjustable floor and wall hanging systems that were adapted from Laura design concepts. This lends a sense of continuity to the Laura

Shoppe division and also takes advantage of the system's flexibility for displaying and merchandising stores.

French limestone, wood veneers, brushed nickel and glass chandeliers all copntribute to the ambiance and suggest the "higher price point." To allow the soft merchandise to be shown off to its fullest advantage, the designers used a palette of creams and taupes combined with color-corrected lighting throughout the space. "Applied with a sense of restraint, these materials and finishes underscore the strong, confident identity of the Melanie Lyne Stores."

In addition, there are numerous focal points to highlight the understated elegance of the space. The central cash/wrap is finished with a cream veneer and highlighted by a pair of custom lamps on top. Rich fabrics were used for the store and fitting room seat upholstery and the intricate ceiling design is accentuated by the custom light fixtures that were used.

PHAT FARM

Prince St., Soho, New York, NY

DESIGN: **Kepron Architect,** Englewood, NJ
David Kepron, AIA
PHOTOGRAPHY: **Eduard Hueber,** New York, NY

Located in Soho, on Prince St., is Phat Farm—a women's sportswear shop that features a collection of urban, classic American clothes. The space, formerly looking like a poorly lit, rustic barn/farmhouse, was turned into something "crisper, more upscale" by the architect/designer David Kepron. The design will eventually work as a vendor shop roll-out.

The new store concept combines two divergent sources: "urban loft" with "country barn." The designer achieved a recognizable look by combining galvanized steel, cold-rolled metals, cherry stained timber, a bio-composite panel made of wheat and an acrylic, back-lit ceiling. Already there and integrated into the new design was a full-height brick wall. "The unique character of the wall was a feature that the client was interested in preserving and so a custom wall mounted fixturing system was designed that would allow for views through open timber frames to the red brick wall beyond."

A metal track runs down the spine of the shop and rolling on it are heavy framed doors which serve as merchandisers, visual panels and space dividers. They help to "restructure the interior to break-out categories of merchandise and present a new space plan to the customer, keeping the store fresh and changing with a seasonal flow of goods." The redesign of the space has increased the merchandise capacity by as much as ten percent with the shelving systems and the flexible floor units that can adapt to variations in merchandise styles. Setting the look for the space and the fixtures are the wide plank, reconditioned timber floors that contrast with, and complement the existing concrete floor up front.

Drawing from the architecture of barn roofs, cherry timbers spring from the face of the wall units that run down the right side of the store and they create the structural system upon which the back-lit acrylic ceiling panels rest. Focusable spots, galvanized metal wall washers and industrial lighting fixtures over the cash/wrap add to the light level of the store and "increase the quality of the visual presentation of the merchandise."

A metal sculpture that was featured in the original store design was salvaged, cut into pieces and reintroduced in the fitting rooms as decorative yet functional hang bars.

SHE

Neuss, Germany

DESIGN: **Inna Dobiasch,** Architect, Munich
and **Vitrashop,** Weil-Am-Rhein, Germany
SHOPFITTINGS & SYSTEMS: **Vitrashop**

THE FASHION DESIGN concept behind "SHE" was to create a modern collection of coordinates suited for today's woman "with her natural, youthful attitude to life, and her high expectations for quality." The company called upon the Munich architect, Inna Dobiasch, who working with Vitrashop—the noted store fittings and systems designers/manufacturers, came up with this "customer friendly" store design that "provides an appealing shopping experience."

The design, as implemented by Vitrashop, consists of various perimeter and mid floor fixtures/fittings which, in effect, create an overall layout which is "clearly defined and uncluttered while also presenting the merchandise to its best advantage." The display units—rectilinear,

flexible and contemporary in style—were designed to complement the light, warm neutral colors of the setting and together they help to "create an overall ambiance which is gentle, clearly defined and very feminine." According to the designers, "The discreet, natural tones of the decor make an ideal background to set off the colors of the fashions on display, ensuring they make the maximum impact on the customer."

The all-glass store front—facing the airport concourse—is used for product display and the giant photo blow-up not only "humanizes" the merchandise shown on the headless forms but it also serves to partially screen off the selling floor from the outside traffic. Inside, the bow of the cash/wrap, located at one side of the store, is emphasized by the sweep of the display cases that lead to the cash/wrap and the dressing room beyond it. Throughout, "functional features are

sophisticated and unobtrusive." Glass shelves are recessed into the rear walls and hanging displays are supported from below—the sliding extensions rest in sockets in the plinth. The fittings consist entirely of simple, geometric structures. "This allows the clothes to take center stage" and the fashion statement is dictated by the design and color of the garments.

The Managing Director, Herbert Loock, said, "We've realized in just the last few months that both our own business—and the retailers who have adopted our strategy of product presentation (in Vendor Shops)—are reaping significant rewards." Good design does pay off!

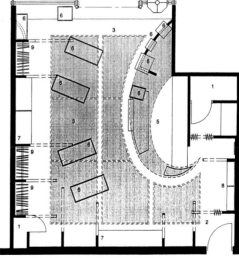

WAREHOUSE

Whiteley's, Bayswater, London, UK

DESIGN: **Caulder Moore,** Kew, UK

THE DESIGN challenge for Caulder Moore was "to ensure consistency across the brand by maintaining the current visual framework and the spirit of the original 'warehouse' loft concept" which was first introduced three years ago. For the new design, shown here, the mandate was "to simplify the design to maintain the contemporary feeling of the store."

The designers simplified some of the key signature architectural details like the skylights and the columns—"in order to modernize the original warehouse-loft concept into a more contemporary loft apartment feeling." A neutral stone floor replaced the original timber one in the design and the floors fixtures were also simplified.

To create a "more sophisticated feeling and communicate a strong customer service ethos" certain areas were introduced or improved. There is now a "lifestyle area" in an alcove across from the cash wrap which serves as a "visual hotspot" and focuses on presenting "on trend" products in depth. Also, the fitting rooms are now more comfortable, softer and welcoming.

To date, this new revised design has been opened in several areas in London as well as in Leeds and Ealing. "The concept is fun, feminine and sexy, building upon the accessibility, friendliness and designer aspirations that define the essence of the Warehouse brand."

BOSS Hugo Boss

Rodeo Drive, Beverly Hills, CA

CONCEPTUAL DESIGN: **Design H. Pummer,** Munich, Germany
PROJECT ARCHITECT: **Brand + Allen, Architects, Inc.,** San Francisco, CA
GENERAL CONTRACTOR: **Fisher Development**
PHOTOGRAPHERS: **Dennis Hearne,** exterior/**Eric Charbonneau,** interiors

THE BOSS Hugo Boss store on Rodeo Drive, in Beverly Hills, follows the conceptual design of Design H. Pummer of Munich which is the signature concept for all BOSS Hugo Boss free standing stores. The project has been realized by the Brand + Allen Arch. firm of San Francisco.
According to the BOSS Hugo Boss organization, "Hugo Boss is a philosophy and a way of life. The world of Hugo Boss is a cosmopolitan world of style, art and design; of sports and glamour; fun and passion; a world of fashion." The same exquisite attention to quality and detail that are the hallmarks of the BOSS Hugo Boss collection went into the design of the retail

space and the setting up of the merchandise.

The exterior has a simple, crisp and clean contemporary facade finished with Indiana limestone outlined with black metal around the windows on both levels and the spacious entrance located under the black BOSS Hugo Boss logo. Additional external light spills into the interior through the giant gridded central window on the upper level.

In contrast, the interior is warm, relaxed and masculine — in a non-threatening way. Large biscuit colored tiles are used to pave the floor and the off-white of the walls and ceiling is complemented by the light, natural woods used to line the recessed wall "wardrobes" as well as finish the simple, contemporary styled floor fixtures. On display on the different levels of the store — the far end of the ground floor is raised up several feet and an inclined ramp plus steps connect the levels — are the BOSS Hugo Boss collection,

sportswear and golf. There is also the Baldessarini Collection which features sophisticated detailing on the elegant clothes. In the rear area of the shop where this collection is housed, patrons and their guests are offered comfortable seating on terra cotta upholstered easy chairs. Giant photo blow-ups of current BOSS Hugo Boss ads add to the vitality of the overall space.

The face-out merchandise is warmly illuminated by MR 16 lamps and pendant lamps are suspended over the cash/wrap counter. The displays in the specially created wall niches are also picked out with highlighting lamps.

KBOND

Los Angeles, CA

DESIGN: **Janson Goldstein,** New York, NY
WITH OWNERS: **Karen Kimmel & James Bond**
PHOTOGRAPHY: **Toshi Yoshimi Photography**

ACCORDING TO THE DESIGNERS of the new Kbond store that recently opened in Los Angeles, "Kbond is about to raise the standard of a man's shopping experience." The store is "immersed in a creative modern environment which will be fully integrated with contextual art." Targeted at consumers who "aspire to a lifestyle of quality," the store has been screened off into three distinct shopping experiences and each one is targeted at a specific aspect of men's dressing. There is a sports and out-of-doors area, a lifestyle sector with brand names "that have stood the test of time or have been reborn or reconsidered for today's man" and the "new method" area where inventive and innovative fashions are the thing.

The 1850 sq. ft., U-shaped shop is the joint vision of the owners—Karen Kimmel and James Bond—and the designers/architects—Mark Janson and Hal Goldstein. "We wanted a place for creative people to come to be able to express themselves creatively," says Bond. James Bond is a believer in the visual and, with the designers, has created a flexible interior that is "art sensitive and interested." The no-color interior has white painted sheetrock walls and polished concrete flooring. Multi-functional, full height fixtures made of medium density fiberboard and translucent scrim fabric are not only used to display the stock of product but they also serve to organize the space into three different zones. According to Hal Goldstein, one of the designers, "Color was the breakthrough and color plays a vital part in defining not only what Kbond is but what is going on in the store." Says Goldstein, "Since Los Angeles is all about the car experience, we wanted to attract the eye—particularly at night." Tinted gels, concealed in the aforementioned scrim covered dividers/fixtures, can trans-

form the entire store till it glows in one of four colors and each color is a visual cue to the Kbond clientele. Red stands for a new delivery of merchandise, green indicates an up-coming event and orange tells shoppers that there is an update on the store's website. When the store is aglow in blue that means that a sale is in progress. Also, alternating colored nylon banners stretched across the display window reinforce the glowing color message during the daylight hours. A "corresponding legend" is sent out to the store's customers to keep them aware of what's playing as well.

Customers are encouraged to touch and feel the merchandise: the flat files encourage shoppers to discover things on their own. To affect a "salon-like" ambiance, as per the owners' request, ottomans are set around that can be used for seating or as display areas to lay-down outfits. The dressing rooms also add a luxurious touch with the parachute silk curtains hung from steel tracks. Small ottoman seats and large mirrors add to the customer comfort in each dressing room. A fun touch is the red rolling cart which is filled with fashion accessories. Goldstein says that it is somewhat like an opened mechanic's tool box.

Adding to the off-beat but definitely pampering ambiance is the purified water system that flows directly out of the wall to cool off the space and the steamer filled with washcloths infused with the aroma of refreshing herbs.

GENTLEMEN'S COURT

Fairview Mall, Toronto, ON Canada

DESIGN: **Burdifilek Design Team,** Toronto, ON
DESIGN DIRECTOR: **Diego Burdi**
MANAGING PARTNER: **Paul Filek**
DESIGNER: **Tom Yip**
PHOTOGRAPHER: **Ben Rahn, Metropoli Pictures,** Brooklyn, NY

GENTLEMEN'S COURT is located in the Fairview Mall in Toronto in a space of 2800 sq. ft. The design challenge to the Burdifilek Design Team, of Toronto, was to create a design that would suggest "the high end haberdashery experience" and would still not intimidate or keep out the cross-section of shoppers in the mall.

According to Ania Szado, speaking for the design firm, "The designers balanced traditional and modern effects to create a calm, masculine retail space suggestive of quality and an upscale lifestyle." The shopper enters through a wide opening that is flanked by a pair of display windows that not only offers a sampling of what is featured inside but a view into the clean, contemporary and masculine space. The walls are mostly white and a pale mauve gray color is used to accent some of the walls. The floor and wall fittings are made of ash and then finished in white or dark chocolate brown. These "anchor the merchandise in a clean, masculine ambiance." The floating, dark brown shelves on some of the white walls show off the neatly folded and lightly stacked sweaters. On one of the mauve tinted walls the shirts are stacked on glass shelves suspended in a wall grid of satin stainless steel pipes. The suits, adjacent, are shown on face-

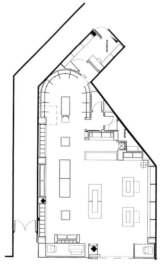

out stainless steel rods supported from above.

"Compartmentalization was key in managing issues of storage and display." The hang bar system was designed so that suits could be shown either face out or shoulder out—

depending upon the stock at any given time. A curved wall, at the rear of the space, leads the shopper to the main suit display. Meanwhile the shopper has had to make his way around the dark stained ash and glass floor fixtures and tables on the beige carpeted floor. The carpet is edged with a border of light ceramic tiles. Located next to the apse-shaped suit area are the dressing rooms and a door leads to the workshop beyond.

The cash/wrap desk is set into a niche in the wall and display cases in the front of the unit show off expensive accessories and jewelry. Incandescent pendant lights and some standing, square shaded lamps complement the warm, color enriching light that emanates from the recessed halogen lamps in the ceiling. Custom rectangular fabric covered "lamp shades" that diffuse the warm incandescent light are suspended over the wood and glass cases set out on the floor.

HUBERT WHITE

Nicollet Mall, Minneapolis, MN

DESIGN: **Smart Associates,** Minneapolis, MN
PRINCIPAL: **Jim Smart**
PROJECT MANAGER: **Janet Whaley**
DESIGNERS: **Jim Smart, Stephanie Reem,
Tijen Roshko**
PHOTOGRAPHER: **George Heinrich,** Minneapolis, MN

FOR ALMOST 90 years Hubert White has been one of Minneapolis' better men's clothing retailers and for 50 of those years the merchandise has been on display in the same location in the historically preserved yet contemporary I.D.S. Building in downtown Minneapolis. The move to an enlarged space of 6,500 sq. ft. brought the Minneapolis based design firm of Smart Associates onto the scene.

"The client's wishes were to maintain the satisfaction and approval of the existing clients while appealing to the younger, more fashion forward clients that had not been exposed to this store in the past because of its 'older executive' image." The space itself is horseshoe in shape with two major entries: one is from the Crystal Court atrium of the building and the other is from a major retail street. Half of the horseshoe has 16 ft. ceilings while the other half soars to 32 ft. Some ceiling elements in the 16 ft. area were raised while dropped elements were added in the higher ceiling area. Some of the drops actually function to contain the HVAC equipment as well as provide high quality lighting in the store.

To attract attention in the Crystal Court, the high traffic shoe department has been placed near that entrance. Through a combination of strong ceiling elements and carpet pattern curves, the designers direct the shoppers through the space and lead them to the sportswear department, into furnishings and the

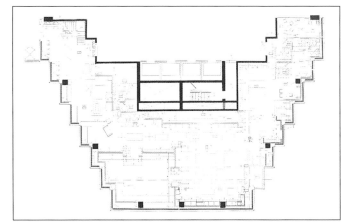

designer clothing shops-within-the-shop and finally into the tailored clothes and fitting rooms. Throughout, the designers combine curves, sweeping arcs and a swirling pattern on the floors and on the ceilings to serve as the directors through the space.

The various areas are unified by the neutral color scheme which is predominantly black, white and gray and these colors not only enhance the merchandise but complement the rich wood used on the floor fixtures. The wood is also used to line some of the wall bays in the designer "shops."

In addition to the effective lighting plan and the use of the dropped ceiling pieces that bring the light down closer to the displayed products, there are many huge windows—especially facing the main shopping street—that allow daylight to stream in. Together, the natural light and the ceiling lights create an open feeling in the store that still has many small "intimate" and "warm" areas.

SEIBU MEN'S DEPARTMENT

Funabashi, Japan

DESIGN: **Callison Architecture,** Seattle, WA
PRINCIPAL IN CHARGE: **Paula Stafford**
DESIGN DIRECTOR: **Sandie Pope**
INTERIORS PROJECT MANAGER: **Cindi Kato**
VISUAL PRESENTATION: **Joseph Cimini**
DESIGNERS: **Elizabeth Buxton & Liz LeDorze**
PROJECT ARCHITECT: **Joel Riehl**

Retailer's Project Team
MILLENNIUM DEVELOPMENT: **Masao Fujikawa**
SEIBU DEPT. STORES: **Toshiaki Matsuhashi & Kazuro Inose**
PHOTOGRAPHER: **Chris Eder,** Seattle, WA

SEIBU DEPARTMENT stores are among the top six department store chains in Asia and one of the most profitable and avant garde in Japan. Callison Architecture, of Seattle, was invited to "help define and implement new retail strategies which would increase brand recognition and position the store as a fashion leader." Working with Millennium Development of Tokyo, the Seibu store in Funabashi was completely redone.

According to William Karst, CEO of Callison, "Attitudes and lifestyles in Japan are changing. To remain competitive Seibu wanted to rethink the way they serve their customers: we're helping them with a long-term repositioning program to achieve their goal." This store was designed with the Seibu customer in mind and the look of the store and the merchandise offered caters to a sophisticated, yet budget conscious lifestyle.

Much of the Men's department is finished in light materials and colors: white walls, white laminates and light natural wood for the wall units, moldings and the trim of the floor units. In some areas there is a preponderance of the light wood on the perimeter wall units and the floor fixtures all of which were designed to be adaptable and flexible. Within the units shelves and hang rods can be altered, display spaces affected and garments can be shown stocked or hung face out or shoulder out. The light maple wood and the grid motif that appear here is also used in other areas of the store as the Seibu brand merchandise identity.

Like most Japanese department stores there are vendor shops with strong individual identities in the store's merchandise mix. Shown here, in a darker wood finish, is one of these shops-within-the-shop in the Men's area.

4 YOU

Kolding, Denmark

DESIGN: **Jorn Hansen AS,** Kolding, Denmark

"IN LINE with current trends, simplicity is a general theme that runs throughout the shop. We have managed to combine this simplicity with a range of experiences and new forms of presentation to give the shop an exciting and inviting atmosphere rather than a cold feel." Thus says Jorn Hansen, the designer and creator of the unique fixturing/fitting systems used in this new 4 You fashion shop in a Kolding shopping center.

The shopper's first impression, upon entering the store, is one of "vast open space." Centered is a

beautiful, round counter constructed of white oak which includes built-in glass display counters for accessory presentations. "More a piece of furniture or sculpture than a counter, it makes a clear statement about the style, purity and simplicity that underpins 4 You's concept and collections."

The store's main fixturing are the wall units which are painted gray with integral glass panels. The underside of the glass has been painted and "this allows the glass panels to create an ever-changing display of colors"— depending upon where the shopper is in the store. 40 mm oak shelves and stainless steel fittings are mounted to the walls. The oak sales counters have steel legs that complement the simple, sleek furniture design. To ensure that 4 You's comprehensive range of accessories is presented at its best, separate areas have been established where they can be shown with

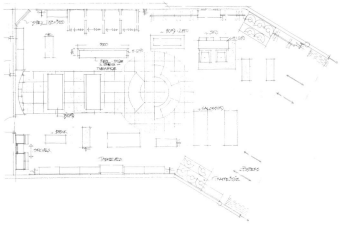

individual centerpiece displays. For the handbags there is an illuminated acrylic wall while a wall of glass paneling supports the watch display. A functional shoe rack unit with integral storage highlights the shoe area.

The 2 You collection is designed to appeal to the "young people" and here the designer used stainless steel and glass fittings that are "extremely minimalist" in their design. The fixtures consist of stainless steel "buttons" mounted directly to the wall with bushings for steel fittings that can serve as shelf supports or be used to hang garments. Double T-stands, also made of steel and glass, are fixed directly to the floor.

To keep the overall space "clean, fresh, raw and yet stylish," the floors are finished with glazed concrete. The image conveyed by the store's design represents "a fine balance between the simplicity of the individual fittings combined with a range of new experiences and the ever changing impressions that customers experience as they move around the shop."

MEN'S WEARHOUSE

Lower Broadway, New York, NY

DESIGN: **The Tricarico Group,** Wayne, NJ

THE VERY LONG (277') but rather narrow (18' 4") space that now houses the Men's Wearhouse on Lower Broadway in New York City presented a problem to the design firm, The Tricarico Group of Wayne, NJ. "The challenge in planning a space that long is how to move the customer to the rear of the space in an engaging and efficient manner while not interrupting the flow of merchandise as well as pedestrian traffic."

The design solution was to organize the space in a "processional sequence" of four different orders of spacial priorities. The entry area, due to the existing ceiling's great height, is now used as a "room" in which a visual merchandising/display statement is made. The ceilings and the arches that span the narrow width are a "gesture" recognizing the neo-Gothic design of the century old landmark building that houses this store. The wrap area, or control point, is located within the main selling area. It too is defined by an arch as one enters and leaves. All the arches—and there are many spanning the long space—have a keystone logo that visually reinforces the

Men's Wearhouse name. The main body of the store or sales area that follows is the "second experience." Here again the arches are used to "visually foreshorten and make the space more inviting to the shopper."

The next zone—the Red Zone—works in tandem with the fitting room area. This is the furthermost area of the store and is articulated differently from the first two areas. In this area the ceilings are pushed up high as they can go "to afford the shopper a place or destination at which to arrive." On the wall of this zone is a 6' x 80' mural that wraps around the space. Done in sepia tones, it depicts the history of the Wall Street area at the turn of the 20th century. Shoes, shirts and ties are on display and stocked here. Turning back toward the front of the store, in a dogleg, is the stock and tailoring area,

which is considered the fourth and final area of the store.

Since this retail shop is located in a landmark building, the designers used the ornate stained glass and leaded glass windows as part of their design concept. The ceiling design took its lead through the expression of these windows on the interior by holding the ceiling four feet away from the lobby and exterior demising walls "in order to capture the already exquisite design within the interior of the Men's Wearhouse space."

"The overall design concept involved one which strives to be in context with the existing architecture as well as incorporating architectura elements and coloration that we already had established for the Men's Wearhouse at prior flagship locations."

TIP TOP TAILORS

Trinity Commons, Brampton, ON, Canada

DESIGN: **Archipole** and **Aedifica,** Montreal, QC
For Archipole:
PARTNER IN CHARGE OF DESIGN: **Robert Bianchi**
ARCHITECT/DESIGNER: **Helene Vallee**

For Aedifica:
ARCHITECT/PARTNER IN CHARGE: **Michel Dubuc**
GRAPHIC DESIGNER: **Stephan Bernier**
PHOTOGRAPHY: **Michel Tremblay**

IN AN EFFORT to depart from the traditional layout and feeling inherent in a typical "big box" store, the architects/designers of this Tip Top Tailors superstore, in Brampton, ON, created a flexible and "unstructured" retail space. Archipole, working with Aedifica, both of Montreal, created a space that "would make a strong impact on consumers but also be relaxed and encourage them to bring their families and stay awhile.

The flagship store has been designed as three zones; the cash wrap up front, the service core with the café and children's play area in the center and the tailor shop and service counter in the rear. The exposed ceiling construction and the light painted walls together with the epoxy finished concrete floors—also

light in color-suggest "an outdoor market "ambiance. The up front cash/wrap desk is surrounded by and highlighted by the colorful display of shirts. The area is simply designed and allows for quick service as well as easy access into the store. Silk screened banners are used at and above eye level to welcome and direct shoppers through the store. The fixtures are set out on the floor in a loose layout so that shoppers can freely move in and around them. Action-posed mannequins float overhead suspended from the metal structures in the ceiling. The bright and open atmosphere is underscored by the metal halide lamps used for the general lighting and the PAR 38 accent lights. To define the service core, canvas tent-like structures are

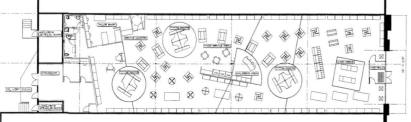

suspended over the area "diffusing light, creating drama and defining the zone." A low gypsum wall, in this zone, provides a back wall for vending machines and the café where non-shoppers can relax, watch TV, or the children in the nearby play area and generally wait in comfort for the shopper to decide.

Two fixturing systems with interchangeable components are used "to create a rhythm along the demising walls." A 12 ft. high system is fixed directly to the wall while a 16 ft. system stands two feet away from the wall. Long vertical standards on the taller system incorporate promotional posters and displays that educate while they also enliven the

space. Supporting the sales strategy are assorted low units, on castors, that are flexible, adjustable and moveable on the floorscape. The MDF and blue painted metal fixtures are simply designed and MDF boxes organize smaller items. Drawers provide quick access on the floor to additional stock. The fitting rooms, usually in clusters of three or four, are also free-standing with two tier fixtures fixed to the end walls for space economy.

To help define the zones and help the clients move through the space, circular carpeted areas of blue stand out from the epoxy coated concrete floors. This store was an award winner in a recent VM & SD / ISP store design competition.

FERRE JEANS BOUTIQUE

Rome, Italy

DESIGN: **Claudio Nardi Architect,** Florence, Italy

THE FERRE JEANS shop, designed by the Florentine architect Claudio Nardi, is located in the Pizza di Spagna. According to the designer, the space is strongly characterized by volumes typical of the old commercial spaces in the Capitoline historic center.

The store window, facing the Piazza, serves to introduce the retail space and the mainly monochromatic merchandise in a sharply defined, minimalist architectural setting. Past the dressed form in the open backed window and the sheer panel with the photographic image, is the ground level of the two level store. Here the fashion accessories are lined up along both long perimeter walls. The staircase, at the very rear of the space, is not only the focal point of this level but it also is the major link between the floors. Men's and women's wear is stocked on the upper level. A giant blue print graphic covers the two story back wall and other blue prints are used throughout the black and white space to add "color."

"Each individual element of the tectonic constituents (giant size photography, wall panels, display tables) strives to be a protagonist yet at the same time elevates the centrality of the visual perspective." They also serve to complement the design of the black ceiling, the

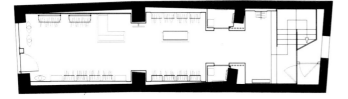

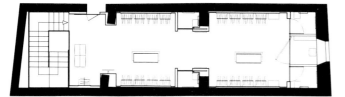

spot light pattern, and the texturing of the large wall panels and the cement effect on the floor.

The monochromatic design is accented by the elegant use of the stainless steel on the staircase. Even the play of the yin/yang of light steps against the wall of the dark steps adds additional interest to the carefully modulated design. The giant photomural is an "abstract" until the whole photo is seen from the second level where the male image looms up to the ceiling.

"The result obtained is a sales space where the strength of the Ferre Jeans image is manifested thoroughly while valuing the pre-existent architectonic scheme, conserving its distinct historical memory of the site."

RALPH LAUREN POLO SPORT

Copley Plaza, Boston, MA

POLO DESIGNERS:
SR. VP, CREATIVE SERVICES: **Alfredo Paredes**
VP STORE DEVELOPMENT: **John Heist**
PROJECT ARCHITECT: **John Hulka**
PROJECT DECORATION HEAD: **Steven Shailer**
PROJECT DESIGN ASSISTANT: **Lee Baratier**

ARCHITECTS: **BAR Architects**, San Francisco, CA

FIXTURES: **555 Manufacturing Inc.,** Chicago, IL
PRESIDENT: **James Geier**
PROJECT MANAGER: **Craig Frase**

PHOTOGRAPHER: **Woodruff/Brown Photographers**,
W. Hartford, CT

THE RALPH LAUREN POLO SPORT 2000 store that opened in Copley Plaza in Boston is an excellent example of how Polo Ralph Lauren, who encompasses a broad range of merchandise that appeals to a vast demographic audience, can target in and focus on one segment of this broad spectrum. The "Sportsman" store in a space of almost 5,000 sq. ft. presents an expanded Polo Sport concept which showcases a unique mix of Ralph Lauren's collection for men and women as well as one-of-a-kind vintage pieces.

Acting as a backdrop for this new retail concept is a modern glass facade trimmed with a thin industrial metal framing. The open look of the shopfront reveals the spacious, loft-like interior which is subtly minimal but still contemporary and very comfortable and inviting. Highlighting the selling space are the 13 ft. gray concrete ceilings and columns, the contrasting crisp white walls and the salvaged hardwood floors. The fixturing by 555 Manufacturing, Inc. of Chicago combines steel and galvanized metal. They echo the "classically contemporary" feeling of the space without being trendy. The lighting comes from the industrial style fixtures suspended from the ceiling.

The eclectic blend of merchandise melds different aspects of the Ralph Lauren lifestyle. Included is a mix of clothing and accessories from Polo Sport, RLX, Polo Jeans, Ralph and a special collection of vintage pieces. "Moveable inspiration boards act as display and merchandising tools giving customers fresh ideas and options to create their own personal style."

DOCKERS

Bluewater Shopping Centre, UK

DESIGN: **Checkland Kindleysides,** London, UK

LOCATED IN the very new and much talked about Bluewater Shopping Centre is this new Dockers store designed by Checkland Kindleysides of London. According to the design firm, " Dockers represents an attitude of life based upon the company's geographical and spiritual home in northern California." To create this image, at either side of the entrance to this shop located in the upper mall there are etched maps featuring the western coastline of the U.S. with details like the name of the states and Dockers' home in San Francisco which is highlighted by a Dockers pants button. The large scale, steel Dockers button set in the floor at the entrance further endorses the brand name and logo. To either side of the opening are large, full height glass windows that give the mall shopper complete access to the store's interior layout and merchan-dise presentation. Frequently changed, large suspended graphic panels are used in the windows to promote as well as show the range and lifestyle imagery of the merchandise.

The interior is light and neutral: natural hardwood floors and wood trimmed floor fixtures, high tech touches in metal in gray and rust as

well as accents of sharp red on the upholstered seating. In the middle of the store, large scale frosted acrylic panels have been introduced in steel frames. They are attached to the floor and ceiling but they are movable. Between these panels, featured garments can be shown along with complementing accessories. This serves as an in-store display window. Situated behind the cash desk is the "Service Statement" which is a 3D display that depicts the alteration service offered in a "quirky" manner. The perimeter walls are lined with assorted height "cabinets" which are divided with shelves into storage and display areas. Some of the larger openings are used

to show face-out hung garments.
Round, tiered floor units show off
stacked garments as do long, rectangular tables.

The focal point, at the rear of the
store, is the "brand wall" which
focuses on eclectic images and
mementos such as club cards, fliers,
tram tickets and maps referring to
north California and the San
Francisco lifestyle.

The halide lamps in the suspended
white baked enamel light fixtures fill
the store with clear, bright ambient
light. Small halogen lamps, on tracks,
are used throughout to accent and
highlight the garments and the displays.

LEVI STRAUSS

Regent St., London, UK

DESIGN: **Checkland Kindleysides Ltd.,** Leister, UK
PARTNER IN CHARGE: **Jeff Kindleysides**
DESIGN TEAM: **Jason West / Kathryn Doverill / Jill Summerfield /**
Carl Murch / Lee Draycott / Ian Jones

THE 10,000 SQ. FT. flagship store for Levi Strauss UK is located on the fast paced Regent St. in London. As designed by Checkland Kindleysides of Leister, it is a totally flexible space. "Every element has been designed to ensure that the store can be redefined and reshaped via movable screens and walls behind which the bulk of the product can be revealed or concealed. The interior of the store has been designed to convey the impression of a large exhibition area."

The store consists of two levels: the ground floor retail space and a lower level. The main entrance facing Regent St. consists of a series of black framed glass doors and a single, open-back window to the left of the entrance which shows off the main selling floor behind the displayed garments.

Throughout the interior the designers have specified lightweight materials including aluminum, rubber and scaffolding fabric work "in synergy with lighting, sound and visual elements." On the main floor products are "concealed" behind fiberglass and nylon, back illuminated membranes. These membranes move to "create access to product and also dedicated concept areas." All the fit-

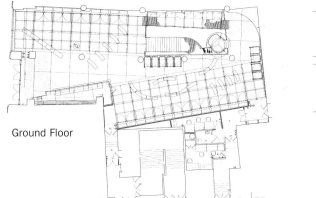

Ground Floor

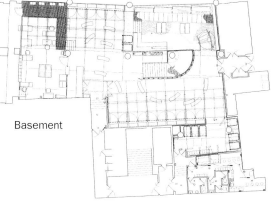

Basement

tings, furniture and even the on-the-floor changing rooms are designed to be moved and rearranged as necessary. Denim is the major product focus on the ground floor and in addition to Men's Denim presentation (on the left) and the cash area (on the right) there is also a general display of the denim product. The cash desk is easily recognized by its translucent blue glass decor. This is a "center of activities" with videos and graphics that "underpin the Levi's craftsmanship in denim" and also shows "the future of denim and artistry through customization."

A stairwell full of strong red color and dazzling high tech materials makes the transition from the ground level to the basement level an experience. Centered in the stairwell is a double-decker DJ tower that not only entertains but puts the source of the entertainment into central focus. A stainless steel and glass bridge dissects the stairway and further

reveals the lower level and the "Chill Out" area. The "Chill Out" space within the stairwell on the lower level was designed to exhibit large-scale art pieces and projections that display upcoming work. Also available in this locale are internet access, books and records.

The Women's area is featured on the lower level along with the "Customize" factory. From a viewing platform shoppers get a bird's eye view of the area where denims can be customized through laser etching, embroidery, abrasion and fabric painting.

The designers have not only created a complete vocabulary of movable fittings but also have added innovations such as the "fit" bar and the "pasta" (lasagna) merchandising principle for showing off the jeans. Instead of being folded or hung on hangers, the pants are draped over a series of dowels that extend out from the graphic covered panel. The pants drape over the rods to affect a lasagna-like look.

According to the designers, "Each element and area has been designed to work in synergy with one another in order to create a retail experience as opposed to a retain environment."

Many of the innovations shown here in the London flagship store were adapted to the Levi flagship store in San Francisco which was also designed by Checkland Kindleysides.

LEVI'S

Vendor Shop in Macy's, Herald Square, New York, NY

DESIGN: **Kepron Architect,** Englewood, NJ
David Kepron, AIA
PROJECT MANAGEMENT: **Sachs Consulting Group,** New York, NY
LEVI STRAUSS & CO.: **Richard Kelly,** Director, Levi's Retail Environment
FIXTURES: **MG Concepts,** Central Islip, NY
PHOTOGRAPHY: **Andrea Brizzi,** New York, NY

I N A 4500 SQ. FT. space with a low ceiling, poor lighting, and large build-outs around existing columns that obstruct clear viewing of the perimeter wall, David Kepron of Kepron Architect of Englewood, NJ was challenged to create a vendor shop for Levi's products in the Macy's Herald Square flagship store. Not only did Kepron have to devise a scheme which would "encourage the customer to venture to the rear of the shop," but he also had to create defined areas for the different groupings of merchandise. "Increasing the light levels to enhance the presentation of merchandise and the creation of a dynamic and unique approach to store fixturing was a directive from the start." Also, a requirement was to incorporate Levi's Original Spin concept into the shop.

The scheme for the overall shop design is characterized by sweeping curves that act as a signature for the

layout of the area, the partition walls, ceiling planes, floor fixtures and wall units. The hard aisle floor pattern is amorphous and is generated from sight lines to feature wall presentation areas. The floor tile lends itself "to the energy of the shop morphing between metallic gray and gold" when viewed from different angles. As a background for the merchandise, translucent fiberglass panels with an upper layer of perforated aluminum foil bent around steel framing was used. They are shaped in a concave curve. "The geometry makes the wall system less imposing and easy to work with ergonomically as well as allowing light from the valence fixtures to rake evenly across the nose of each shelf."

A large curved wall stretches across the rear of the space and it separates the

selling areas from the fitting rooms behind. Crushed aluminum panels, fastened with Levi's copper rivets, cover the wall that is also a major focal point in the overall design. The doors to the fitting rooms are surfaced with linticulars that transform between Levi's Red Tab logos and lifestyle photography as the doors swing open or as the shopper walks by. Motion sensors in the fitting rooms turn on the lights and music pours down from a listening dome mounted in the ceiling.

A shallow vault of metal mesh was used between the beams to conceal the existing ceiling that was "a complex weave of building structure." Fluorescent ceiling fixtures hang below this metal vault to reflect light off the curves onto the selling floor. In addition, the architect/designer included uplighting and cove lighting on the ceiling and a perimeter wall valence light system that makes this formerly dark area bright and inviting.

LEVI'S JEANS FOR WOMEN

Macy's, Herald Square, New York, NY

DESIGN: **Morla Design**, San Francisco, CA.
ART DIRECTOR AND DESIGNER: **Jennifer Morla**
ASSOCIATE CREATIVE DIRECTOR: **Brian Collins,** FCB/Levi Strauss
ART DIRECTOR: **Eric Rindal,** FCB/Levi Strauss
PHOTOGRAPHY: **Sheila Metzner**

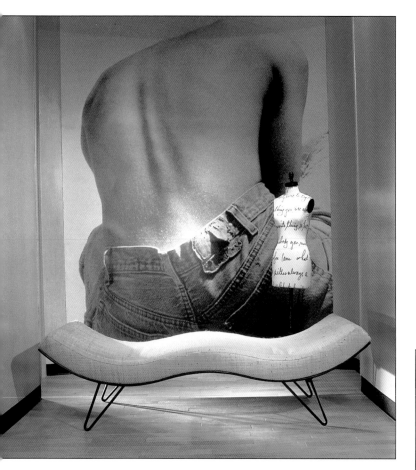

THIS UNIQUE shop-within-the-shop for Levi's Jeans for Women was built in a 3,200 sq. ft. space in Macy's Herald Square flagship store in NY. The target market is women between the ages of 15 and 30.

The designer, Jennifer Morla of Morla Design, working very closely with the creative talents of FCB/ Levi Strauss, based the design concept of the store on "shape." The "shape" that is reinterpreted over and over is the soft sensuous curve — curves like on a woman's body. Laminated glass walls curve, convex and concave, to create hallways and passageways while photographic murals show the female body against "curvaceous"

sandstone rocks. The wave-like, custom designed benches follow through on the shape concept as well.

One of the more graphically exciting ideas is the use of cursive script scrawled in off white on charcoal black carpeting which is laid on the floor in front of the cash wrap and in the changing area. The script is based on "entries one might find in a woman's diary or journal." The script not only reaffirms the soft, curve motif but it also adds a personal touch to the otherwise neutral space. Custom fabric, with the same cursive script, is used to upholster some of the many different shaped and sized dress forms that are set around the space as decorative elements. They do not carry merchandise; they do carry through the shape message.

The jeans are neatly stacked in neutral wood cubicles that are built into the perimeter walls. They are outlined and accented with matte black finishes. The floor tables are made of the same wood. Where the floors are not covered with the carpet, natural colored wood was used.

The floating ceiling of the focus area accents the benches upholstered in the golden beige, rough-textured fabric as well as the furniture and the softly fluted lighting fixtures.

NAPA

Guadalajara, Mexico

DESIGN: **Ares Arquitectos,** Guadalajara, Mexico
ARCHITECT: **Jacinto Arenas**

THE CLIENTS wanted the new Napa casual menswear store to have the spirit and attitude of the Napa Valley in California. Since the merchandise offering was not "traditional" but tended towards trendsetting fashions, the designer felt that the Napa ambiance should be more sophisticated and stylish rather than "realistic."

The design firm created an open wood structure with simulated beams on top that ended at the slice of white ceiling that runs the length of the space. The adjustable lighting fixtures are attached here and they illuminate the merchandise displayed on the perimeter wall. The white ceiling is enhanced by the dark areas to either side—seen through the network of the beams. The two long perimeter walls are divided into adaptable bays by the vertical timbers that angle away, at approximately ten feet off the floor, to reach the light filled ceiling. This creates a smart looking "barn-like" setting. The fixturing system design is very flexible with recessed standards used that can accommodate shelves and/or hang rods "because the client wanted the freedom of exhibiting the merchandise as loosely as possible." To make up for the height of the space, Arenas used the area above the stock for display arrangements and grommeted canvas graphics and signage which are lashed into the frames formed by the crossing of the vertical and horizontal beams.

The flooring is natural concrete with inlaid strips of wood that not only tend to enhance the width of the long and narrow store but also break it up into a series of spaces. To keep the look of the store consistent, the designer also designed the "folding/hanging" gondolas and the simple display tables made of the same wood used on the walls. In

addition to the warm, focusable spots above there are three steel hanging lamps, designed by Ares Arquitectos.

The store's facade is set on an angle to the main aisle and one wall has been painted lavender to recall the focal panel at the far end of the store. Here, too, it is used as a display area—up front and on the aisle. The entrance design is an irregular grid of the same timber used within, and it introduces the barn construction-updated-motif. The same lashed-in canvas lifestyle graphics are shown here while the Napa sign is set into a long, diamond shaped frame and it is illuminated from within.

TREASURES & TRADITIONS

St. Augustine, FL

DESIGN: **Pavlik Design Team,** Ft. Lauderdale, FL
PRESIDENT/CEO: **Ronald J. Pavlik**
PROJECT DESIGNER: **Patricia Dominguez**
PROJECT MANAGER: **Jon Hart**
LIGHTING DESIGNER: **Sven Pavlik**

WITH "MEMORABILIA"—or just plain souvenirs—a big business, it was only natural that there should be an exit shop located in the World Golf Hall of Fame building in St. Augustine, FL. Pavlik Design Team of Ft. Lauderdale was commissioned to create a retail environment which would integrate both commemorative merchandise with apparel.

The designers conceived a plan that would reflect a series of events—points of interest that would "lead the visitor on a path of factual discovery and merchandise awareness." According to the designer, "The layout of the dioramas and their stories lead people through the various offerings related to both the period's history and the display's story." Along the various

pathways there are large scale models of historical and memorable golf courses. To support the shop being part of the Golf Hall of Fame, encircling the store are insightful and often humorous quotes from golfing greats. Digiprint vinyl wall coverings illustrate the graphic quotes.

Along with the memorabilia there is an apparel shop within the shop where golfing clothes are on sale. Warm cherry wood floor fixtures and wall units carry the merchandise and the overall neutral color scheme is gently accented by the soft green marble tiles that suggest the rolling greens of golf courses. The same rich wood is combined with the polished beige stone on the floor. Enhancing the overall ambiance and the assorted classifications of merchandise is the well planned and executed lighting design that fills the space with rich, warm light.

L.L. BEAN

Tysons Corner Center, McLean, VA

ARCHITECT/DESIGNER: **Callisom Architecture,** Seattle, WA
ASSOCIATE PRINCIPAL: **Sandie Pope**
DESIGN PRINCIPAL: **Doug Stelling**
PROJECT DESIGNER: **Christine Chaney**
PROJECT MANAGERS: **David Heinen & Ryan Phelps**
ENVIRONMENTAL GRAPHICS: **Joan Insel**
INTERIOR DESIGN: **Stephanie Long**
PROJECT ARCHITECT: **Mark Sharp**

In-House Design Team, L.L.Bean:
DIR. OF RETAIL MERCHANDISING & BRANDING: **Mike Verville**
MNGR. OF CREATIVE DIRECTION & RETAIL DESIGN
DEVELOPING: **Paul Maddrell**
SR. PROJECT MANAGER: **J.D.Scheckenberg**
RETAIL DESIGN DEVELOPMENT SPECIALIST: **Judy Hamlin**
MNGR. OF RETAIL MARKETING: **Rita Armstrong**
RETAIL GRAPHIC ART DIRECTOR: **Wendy Graham**

FIXTURES: **Met Merchandiser/Maine Woodwork &
Design/M. Lavine Design**
LIGHTING: **Denise Fong, Candela**
PHOTOGRAPHY: **Maxwell MacKenzie,** Washington, DC

THE NEW, 76,000 SQ.FT., two-level L.L. Bean store located in Tyson's Corner Center in McLean, VA, is a prototype for a "new generation of retail stores" which will bring the famous catalog company noted for its outdoor and apparel equipment into malls across the country. The original Freeport, ME, store and the L.L. Kids shop nearby have been major attractions for visitors and shoppers in Maine and now with this store, designed by Callison Architecture of Seattle, the company introduces another type of retail setting that still carries on the founders' original philosophy of presenting simple, honest and straightforward products to the public.

According to the design firm, "The straightforward personality of Bean's trademark 'Boat & Tote' bag guided the design." Sandie Pope, designer at Callison's said, "We want the customers to come into a friendly familiar environment that presents the merchandise in a clear, practical way that we may refer to as 'smart like the bag.'"

"The products have evolved over time and so should their store environment. The most important thing is the product, so that's the main thing you see when you're in the store—not the architecture and trees and the knotty pine."

Reminiscent of New England architecture is the store's facade with its stained clap-board siding and timber framed clerestory which rises above the roof. Light enters not only through the clerestory openings but through the expansive glass curtain wall of the facade. Altogether they create a high ceilinged space

for the outdoor gear merchandise. A wooden trellis, over the mall entry, signals the transition from outdoors to indoors. Inspired by the plan of a New England seacoast village, inside the store pathways are suggested that lead the shoppers to the various merchandise zones and the feature areas that feel like shops-within-the-store —but all under one roof.

The interior finishes, fixtures and graphics "support the contemporary translation of the L.L. Bean brand." The merchandise steps forward from the clean, neutral surrounding palette and the feature areas are readily changed seasonally. Throughout there is natural finished wood on the feature columns, the suspended trellis elements and the ceiling

rafters. The recurring trellis sets a theme as it appears in front of brightly painted feature walls as entries to different shops or areas. The flooring materials vary from area to area: wood planking, rusticated stone, rubber and cork tiles. The different flooring materials help to distinguish the various merchandise categories and "communicate different aspects of the products." In the apparel area the narrow wood planking suggests the inside of a cabin while the dark green rubber flooring is so appropriate for the outdoor sports gear displayed in that zone.

Some of the iconic elements found in the Freeport store are recreated here. There is the pond stocked with live trout, the 16 ft. waterfall, a climbing wall for children and a stone hiking ramp. These elements are part of what has made the Freeport store such an attraction. In addition, there is an honest-to-goodness sense of authenticity about the store's design. "If Bean is based on honesty and simplicity in its product, then we shouldn't build an over dense store that recreates some place in an amusement park. It is not entertainment retail. It is about selling product," says Ms. Pope.

Additional "core" stores—like this new design—are scheduled to be rolled out in the New England and Mid-Atlantic states. Smaller stores—"discovery stores"—of about 30,000 sq. ft. will also be developed and the first is scheduled to open soon in Columbia, MD.

MACYSPORT

W. 34th St., New York, NY

DESIGN: **Chute Gerdeman,** Columbus, OH

MACY'S FLAGSHIP store on 34th St. and Broadway in Manhattan has recently opened its new MacySport. Chute Gerdeman of Columbus, OH was asked by the Federated Stores to design the 15,000 sq. ft. activewear store in the lower level of the store. The undertaking was to develop new initiatives that would attract younger shoppers who have over the years gravitated towards specialty stores like the ones that now surround Macy's. To set the look and to attract this younger demographic group—the older ones will follow—MacySport has its own distinctive facade and a separate off-the-street entrance. The giant graphics and attractive signage make an immediate appeal. The new entrance is on 34th St.—facing the competition, the traffic and the potential customers. A 30' x 10' vertical billboard features an athlete in action and a flash-

ing L.E.D. readerboard displays the latest scores and information on upcoming sporting and special events. From this entrance shoppers descend into a "total sports" environment. Here, Macy's becomes the new fashion authority on Sports with an expanded merchandise mix featuring the best brands in sports apparel, equipment, and accessories presented in a visually exciting layout with futuristic fixtures backed up by dynamic and exciting graphics. According to Kevin Morrissey, Exec. V.P./General Merchandise Manager, Men's of Macy's East, "It's a total sensory experience and it caters to the casual and serious athlete by bringing them the premier names in apparel and accessories."

The space is laid out on an elliptical track with sport specific and vendor shops springing off from the central space. The futuristic feeling of the store

is generated by the palette of cool blue, steel gray and olive punctuated with bright neon orange and cobalt blue which is used for the MacySport logo. The clean, modern look is industrial and accentuated by the use of perforated metal and aluminum on the walls and the colored, glazed concrete floors. The designers have used effective elements of design to create the balance between sports and fashion by introducing curved walls, arcs, bends and dropped curved fascias as well as strong, three dimensional signage placed above eye-level. The fixtures are high tech/urban in styling with perforated metals, steel mesh, aluminum pipes and big wheels to make the floor units easy to arrange and rearrange. The adaptable fixtures combine hanging with shelving plus face out displays and they are compatible with the wall systems.

Each area is visually identified by the graphics used to enhance the selling floor. The graphics feature vignettes that capture the athlete in a personal moment of his or her sport. Two video walls—jammed full of TV monitors—show live feeds of sporting events and fashion presentations from some of the vendors represented in the store: Nike, Adidas, Puma and The North Face. "Gobo's" (computer generated slide visuals) add to the non-stop action in the space with images and noted logos bouncing on and off the nine columns while flashes of changing colors, spinning fashion and sports images and brand I.D.'s all enhance the sense of action and excitement.

To make this a "must see/must shop" destination, hot names in sports and style—for men and women—are shown here. The merchandise ranges from traditional sports such as soccer and basketball to some of the new "in" things such as rollerblading, snowblading, skateboarding and cycling. MacySport inte-

grates all areas of activewear from footwear, sport watches, and sunglasses to outdoor apparel and sport specific clothing and gear. Each sport specific shop has knowledgeable salespeople that not only know the merchandise but the sport itself. They are equipped to give the best fashion and accessory advice relevant to the sport.

The executives of Macy's East expect female shoppers to account for almost a quarter of the activewear sales in MacySport. "We created MacySport so the female shopper will feel comfortable. She won't feel like she's in a sporting goods store. With the images of females (in the graphics) we think the customer will respond. She will find it inviting instead of intimidating," said Kevin Morrissey. In keeping with that idea, Morrissey continues, "We always have an edge on fashion with a technical turn to it. Fashion is what will drive our business."

LIMITED TOO

Tuttle Crossing, Columbus, OH

DESIGN: **Limited Store Planning, Inc.,** Columbus, OH
VICE PRESIDENT: **Debbie Urton**
DIRECTOR: **Mark Askew**
SR. CONSTRUCTION MGR.: **Dan Tompkins**
SR. DESIGNER: **Charlie St. Clair**
DESIGNER: **Stephan Calhoun**
VISUAL PRESENTATION DIRECTOR: **Connie Meizlish**
PHOTOGRAPHER: **Antoine Bootz,** NY

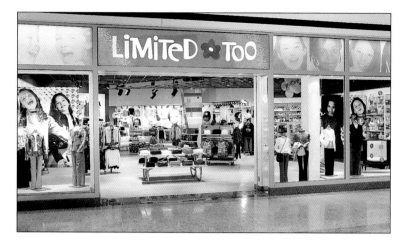

TO CREATE this new mall destination for girls aged ten to thirteen, the design team at The Limited's Store Planning division studied that market: their likes and dislikes; their dreams and aspirations. The resulting concept is an environment that is "her place" — a place to shop, meet friends, hangout and gossip. It is a "clubhouse" for pre-teens that is designed to be "whimsical, curious, high energy and stimulating for her senses."

The open glazed facade shows off the bright colors and patterns that enliven and contribute to the fun attitude of the space. Included are the giant photo blow-ups of the targeted customer. The floor is mainly maize yellow with splashes of tomato red in the seating and fitting areas. Visible through the suspended apple green grid is the dark blue painted open ceiling. The primary focus is the curved curtain wall or "screen" that has

projected images and/or a theatrical light
show. A support column has been turned
into a multi-colored/multi-patterned mosaic tile caprice with elements of water, sky,
grass and daisies scattered on it.

Really important to the girls of the des-
ignated age group is the telephone and
thus the telephone is introduced into the
store's design. There are phone booths
encrusted with colorful stickers, labels,
messages and numbers where girls can
either talk to their friends at another
phone booth in the store or use the phones
as music stations for specially piped in
programs. The store's "signature sound"
(created by AEI Music of Seattle) is Hip
Hop, R&B, Pop and Swing.

Throughout there are fun and familiar
objects and symbols introduced decorative-
ly or as part of the fixture design. They are
used to enhance the shopper's visit and to
encourage return visits. There are the
aforementioned phone booths, gum ball
machines, "flower power" cut-outs and
appliques, pink curtains in the dressing
rooms and funky vinyl covered chairs in
yellow and aqua. Who wouldn't want to
rest on a hassock completely covered with

small, cuddly teddy bears? They set up of
the fitting area encourages interaction
between friends shopping together. The
wall paper in this area is patterned with
blocks of bright overlapping colors and the
assorted shaped hanging lights look like
refugees from the '50s and '60s. All this
adds up to a Limited Too total experience.

VELVET PIXIES

Rockaway Townsquare, Rockaway, NJ

DESIGN: **FRCH Design Worldwide,** Cincinnati, OH
PRINCIPAL, INTERIOR DESIGN: **Paul Leichleiter**
PRINCIPAL, GRAPHIC DESIGNER: **Tessa Westermeyer**
GRAPHIC DESIGNER: **Jenny Kerr**
GRAPHIC PRODUCERS: **Liz Tefend, Jeff Waggoner**
DESIGNER: **Rebekah Fellers**
VISUAL MERCHANDISER: **John Frederich**
STRATEGIST: **Rebecca Stillpass**
COLORS & MATERIALS: **Lori Koltoff, Maggie Schmidt**
PROJECT MANAGER: **Paul Haqrlor**
COMNSTRUCTION DOCUMENTATION: **Keith Witt**

FOR THE CLIENT: **Claire's Stores,** Pembroke Pines, FL
SR. V.P. CLAIRE'S BOUTIQUES: **Marla Schafer**
PHOTOGRAPHER: **Peter Paige,** Upper Saddle River, NJ

VELVET PIXIES is a new retail concept developed by FRCH Design Worldwide of Cincinnati, OH for Claire's Inc., a retail group. The new concept is a "fashion forward, trend-driven, fantasy based retail destination" for seven to 12 year old girls. The shop features private label apparel, accessories and gear targeted at "urban and urbane young girls with spending power." Working with the management of Claire's, Inc., FRCH created the prototype store in a 2600 sq. ft. space in a mall in Rockaway, NJ. Together they evolved the branding and positioning strategy for the new concept and the playful and colorful interior was designed as a lifestyle and fashion club/hangout.

The Pixie Path is the store's main traffic aisle and strewn across the dyed and stained concrete floor are words written in "a child's hand" that might have been lifted from a girl's diary. Text from the "diary" is digitally printed on wallpaper that is wrapped around the structural columns. Pinks and purples dominate on the wall area in the paints and papers used while yellows and green dominate in the laminates used on the fixtures. Textures are important in this scheme and shiny vinyls contrast with velvety fabrics. The fun continues with the design elements as well. The signature wall fixture is an oversized "Barbie" style doll case lined with tufted vinyl. These cases are set along the perimeter wall "to effectively present

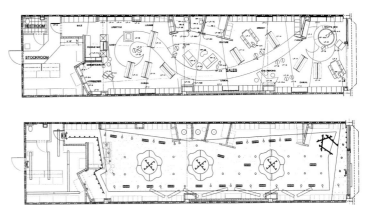

the changing collection of fashion ensembles ranging from 'Sunday best' to casual, active and sleep wear." A highlight of the shopping experience is a visit to the changing rooms which resemble shower stalls. Ceramic tiles outline each "stall" and vinyl shower curtains provide some privacy. Bathroom style hardware is used for hanging garments and a standard pendant light fixture was used because it resembles a shower head. To further that imagery, the light fixture is wrapped with copper tubing and the suspended crystals suggest dripping water.

Since shopping Velvet Pixies is supposed a social and shared experience, there are couches located near the changing rooms for friends or parents who wait. The "Poodle Bar" is the cash/wrap counter where makeup and toiletries are displayed. The counter resembles a kid-sized diner. The ear piercing station, up

front, takes place at a frilly, feminine dressing table.

The graphics that were especially designed for Velvet Pixies include the Pixie Girls. They are reproduced on vinyl and applied on the traffic aisle, on the mannequins and on the walls. Appearing on stickers, gift bags and shopping bags are butterflies, hearts, stars and flowers. The designers also created fashion tip cards, hatboxes, price and promotion cards as well as custom sign holders. "Part fantasy, part edge, part fun. This place serves up the right music, the right attitude and the right stuff. This is your time, live your life. What are you waiting for? "The Velvet Pixies is waiting for you!!

ATOM & EVE

Toronto, ON, Canada

DESIGN: **II x IV Design Associates,** Toronto, ON
PHOTOGRAPHY: **David Whittaker**

THE RETAILERS/OWNERS of Atom & Eve identified the lack of high quality, well made and fashionable shoes for the infants to pre-teen market. Equipped with sources for such products in Italy and Spain, a prime mall location and the expert design firm, ll X lV Design Associates of Toronto—they were off.

The name is expressed in a logo that combines apples and atomic symbols. It first appears with several dimensional apples on the translucent header panel over the wide open shop front and reappears, inside, along with the component words in the Boys and Girls areas. Off to one side of the store opening is a big, shiny red apple with a child-size cut out doorway in it through which children are invited to enter the store. On the back side of the large, dimensional apple one can see the flesh and seeds. The apple reappears throughout the store as a decorative motif. A large photo blow-up of green apples backs up the cash/wrap desk which, like the store's display windows, is fitted with small cubicles in which featured styles are shown. Above small carpeted areas, to either side of the main aisle, a cove-recessed ceiling is revealed. Mobiles dangle down from the sky-blue center and the green apples of the mobile seem to be falling into and collecting in bowls of real apples that are located below on display cubes.

The cubes are constructed of MDF painted with a shiny white epoxy and they are flanked by lower benches upholstered in taupe and copper colored fabrics. The circle motif of the fabric coordinates with the pattern on the carpet and they recall the apple theme. Other white, epoxy finished benches, lit from below, highlight the featured designs. A rich, cherry wood color is used to complement the white "jelly bean" shaped displayers and the same color plastic laminate sheaths the walls and works with the wall merchandising system. The panels also conceal the lighting system that creates the edge lit pattern on the plexiglass shelves that are extended off of the panels. More acrylic topped display benches glow beneath the cherry panels and mirrors below them add sparkle and light to the scene,

The back wall features a giant photo of green apples flanked by oversized, back-lit images on active boys and girls. Below is a large TV monitor where videos and cartoons amuse the children while the moms and dads do the actual shopping. The children can either sit on the carpeted floor or rest on the assort-

ed benches which they have to share with a menagerie of stuffed toy animals. A game-board-like pattern on the vinyl floor with the extra wide aisles, makes this a welcoming store for parents, baby carriages and free-running children.

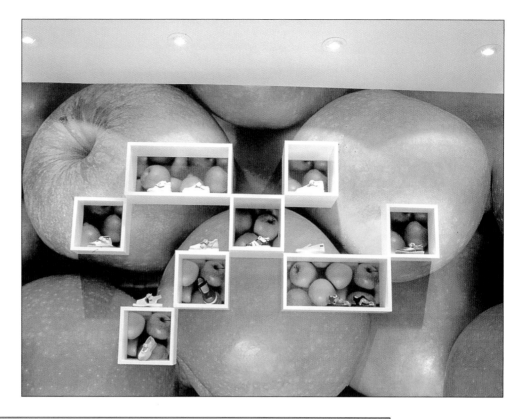

COQUETA

Galeria del Calzado, Guadalajara, Mexico

DESIGN: **Area Arquitectos,** Guadalajara, Mexico
ARCHITECT: **Jacinto Arenas**

THE GALERIA DEL CALZADO is a mall in Guadalajara that is devoted entirely to the sale of shoes. The Coqueta shop, designed by the Guadalajara-based Ares Arquitectos takes up about 650 sq. ft. and was created as a prototype for the children's shoe retailer.

To make the store attractive to chil-

dren and also to distinguish it from the shoe stores surrounding it, Jacinto Arenas, the architect/designer, combined whitewashed wood floors with maple wood and bright primary colors. The physical space is broken up by areas of color: light yellow, lime, aqua and a feature wall that combines a sharp blue with the maple wood set against a sky blue wall. Highlighting the wall are the assorted shaped boxes lined in orange and lime green. Featured shoes are presented in these color-highlighted areas while others are show "walking" across walls on invisible glass shelves supported by invisible fittings.

The designer has filled the space with interactive materials for the children to play with such as an inset "abacus" under a line of shoes on the lemon yellow wall and the convoluted and fun swirling wire contraption with colored beads begging to be moved up and down and around the many curves. In addition to the two round

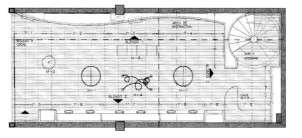

maple seating "poufs" there is a rectangular bench. All are enlivened with pillows of orange, yellow, lime and blue. A half round, lime green sheathed cash/wrap is set into a corner of the space.

The facade was designed to be as open as possible to entice and encourage shoppers to enter. There is a transparent display area to the right of the entrance and it introduces the theme of the store's design: elementary shapes and forms combined with bright and clear colors—plus maple wood. The sinuous curving wall on the left moves the shoppers toward the rear of the space and the amusing clock on the wall where children can tell their own time. Throughout, light played a key role in the design. Compact fluorescents were used for the general light and HQIs for the general perimeter lighting. MR16s and superspots provided the highlights and accenting. A haze of blue fluorescent lighting emanates from below the dropped ceiling plane and that adds further interest to the small space.

STUARTS-KANTER

Coral Gables, FL

DESIGN: **Echeverria Design Group,** Coral Gables, FL

FOR OVER 30 YEARS Stuarts-Kanter has successfully served several generations of Coral Gables families. The 1700 sq. ft. children's shoe store with a 600 sq. ft. mezzanine was given a new look by the Echeverria Design Group, also of Coral Gables. "Our intention," says Mario Echeverria, the designer, "was to increase the fundamental selling area, shoe stock capacity and at the same time design a functionally efficient space without diminishing the store's established product appeal."

The storefront was projected out to create a dynamic entranceway and make the store a "visual display showcase." That simultaneously created valuable merchandising space while reducing the original area for stock. The volume of the non-selling area storage was increased by introducing mobile shelving units on both levels of the store. Additional storage is on the selling floor contained in the colorful nesting blocks that also serve as display platforms. Also adding to the storage volume are the perimeter wall units introduced that accommodate both upper and lower storage compartments.

Light maple wood veneers combined with primary colors "create a shopping experience without being overly bold."

By the clever and attractive use of colors, shapes, textures and the overall effective lighting plan, the ambiance appeals to children and parents alike. Blue glass shades are suspended from the dropped ceiling to enhance the residential scale of the space and make it seem more in scale to the children's products. The heavily trafficked central seating area is carpeted with 18" x 18" carpet tiles of assorted colors. They are easily replaced when worn or stained. To keep the children amused and distracted while the parents shop, a video monitor shows cartoons. In addition, the designer introduced soft, sweeping curves "to convey a sense of continuity." There are curved and grid shaped elements that appear as ellipses on both the floor and the ceiling above and the curves are architecturally projected onto the column entryway and storefront to "create a sense of motion."

The designer not only satisfied the client's requirements but exceeded the client's original vision. The new Stuarts-Kanter store is now ready to serve generations to come.

COACH

Madison Ave. and 57th St., New York, NY

DESIGN: **S. Russell Grove**, New York, NY
PROJECT MANAGER: **Daniel Wismer**
PHOTOGRAPHY: **Sharon Risendorph**, San Francisco, CA

LOCATED ON the prestigious corner of Madison Ave. and E. 57th St. in NYC in the landmark Fuller Building is the new, 6,500 sq. ft. Coach store. For the new concept, the designer, S.Russell Grove, sought "to highlight Coach's position as a classic American leather goods design house." The inspiration for the three-level store came from the 1940 "Industrial Aesthetic" of Coach's original factory.

A 20' x 20' quadrant was removed from each floor, creating a light filled volume connects the three floors of merchandise. The glazed brick that spans one side of the resulting geometric "atrium" is used for the presentation of enlarged fashion images and product display. It also serves as a backdrop for the nickel and concrete, open riser staircase that links the levels.

The fixtures that were designed for this store are "modern and geometric" and they were produced with indigenous American materials such as milk painted pine and mahogany. Added to this are "early modern industrial materials" such as ribbed glass and nickel. In keeping with the overall look and theme, the flooring reinforces the industrial mood with monochromatic concrete and end block wood.

The storefront is matte black intumescent painted steel highlighted with brushed nickel signage. An extra "friendly" touch is the three part canopy over the entrance made of sunbrella natural canvas. On street level, the open brushed nickel tube railings of the open staircase makes a strong visual statement in the almost all white setting. Here, the floor is ebonized Douglas fir end block and the stair treads are custom color ardex in brushed nickel pans. The cabinetry is constructed of flat cut mahogany and snow white milk paint on plain sliced pine. The cash wrap counter is topped with starphire glas, back painted white. All the leather furniture in the comfort-

Entry Level

Mid Level

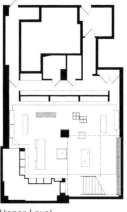

Upper Level

able seating areas are by Coach and feature the fine Coach leathers for the upholstery. The clusters of upholstered chairs and sofas are defined by the looped, natural linen area rugs.

Throughout there is a feeling of intimacy and warmth even though the 1940-ish modern lines dominate. The merchandise is presented with great restraint and true elegance on white lacquered steel fixtures topped with ribbed Bendheim glass. The cool blue color of the glass is picked up in the wall cubicles as an accent for the handbags. "The materials and detailing of the project unify the design while the distinct natural light conditions give each floor a specific mood, reacting to the product categories."

The overall result is a clean modern space, "combining a dramatic spacial sequence with crisp detailing."

CHARLES JOURDAN

Champs Elysees, Paris, France

CONCEPT: **Rena Dumas Architecture Interieure,** Paris, France
REALIZATION: **Vitrashop, S.A.R.L.,** Paris, France
PHOTOGRAPHY: **Adriano A, Biondi,** Basle

WITH THE NEW millennium, Charles Jourdan introduced its "2000 Years" concept. Following the company's policy of integrated distribution, there are now store outlets ringing the world: from Kuwait, Dubai, Valencia, Moscow, Hamburg and London to all around the U.S. In its flagship store, located on the prestigious Champs Elysees in Paris, the recent renovation was undertaken under the direction of Rena Dumas, a noted Parisian interior designer. The elegant old house "represents the timeless elegance values of the brand."

The shoes, bags and fashion accessories as well as some of the firm's ready-to-wear garments are displayed in a warm, neutral setting. The off-white walls and ceiling are complimented by the white sycamore wood wall paneling and the cabinetry produced by Vitrashop, a fitting/system designer-manufacturer with an office in Paris. Peach and coral upholstered chairs, poufs and settees are scattered around the open and spacious shop and like the walls and cabinetry, they are complemented by the subtle gray carpeting underfoot.

The designer has introduced merchandise carrying wall partitions and shelved cabinets that almost reach the ceiling to divide the space into more intimate, interesting and product focused areas. In the long rear end of the shop—away from the windows that open on to the Champs Elysees—the run of white sycamore panels and wall units are sinuous in design. The step-up design of the undulating wood

serves to show off the shoes while the glass shelves in the wavy wall cabinets show off more shoes, bags and small accessories. In contrast to the "moving" walls, white marble areas surround and accentuate the rectangular areas of carpeting. Tilted, eight foot tall mirrors on stainless steel bases rise up not only to offer the client a place to see herself but to reflect more of the sparsely set out products.

Overhead, the ceiling is filled with focusable, recessed lamps that provide the ambient light as well as highlight the wall held merchandise. Product themes are developed in the various Vitrashop fixtures "which highlight the product rather than the display system."

MARTINEZ VALERO

Third Ave., New York, NY

DESIGN: **Zivkovic Associates Architects,** New York, NY
PROJECT TEAM: **Don Zivkovic, Hugh Higgins, Brian Connolly**
LIGHTING DESIGN: **Gary Gordon**
PHOTOGRAPHER: **Ashley Ranson,** Toronto, Canada

THE FLAGSHIP store of Martinez Valero, the Spanish couture footwear manufacturer, is located on the corner of E. 61 St. and Third Ave. in NY. It is very close to Bloomingdale's and the designer boutiques on Madison Ave. The 680 square foot space is on the ground level of a high rise tower and there is an additional 650 square foot of space in the basement for offices, storage and toilets.

According to Don Zivkovic of the design firm Zivkovic Associates Architects, "the layout and the general design of the store is intended to highlight the merchandise with minimal background distractions to divert the customer's attention." To accomplish this, the design team worked

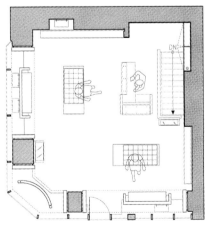

with a limited palette of light colors materials: a gray carpet and white walls and ceiling. Sycamore-veneered panels and matching custom millwork provide a warm contrast "while adding detail, intimacy of scale and sophistication."

This neutral background serves the shoes and bags on display.

Only a sales desk and two low benches are placed within the interior space. The patternless carpet extends to all of the perimeter walls thus isolat-

ing these free standing elements loosely within the interior. "Both window conditions are framed with over-scaled portal constructions providing elements of grandeur in the diminutive space." These, in turn, enclose—proscenium-like—the display units at the window locations.

Sycamore veneered panels framed within matching portal enclosures are used in the window to restrict views of the interior from the sidewalk. Cantilevered glass shelves against the sycamore panels are used to display—museum-like—a very select inventory of shoe styles.

GIROUX

South Beach, Miami, FL

DESIGN: **Blitstein Design Associates,** Coral Gables, FL
PRINCIPASSL IN CHARGE: **Peter Blitstein**
PHOTOGRAPHY: **Dan Forer,** Miami, FL

TRENDSETTING and very fashionable Collins Ave. in South Beach, Miami is the setting for this surprising and simply-elegant Giroux shop. In this 1800 sq.ft. prototype design in the heart of South Beach is a collection of shoes culled from all over the world including original designs with the Giroux label.

"The overall concept," according to the designer, Peter Blitstein, "was to leave as much of the original texture as possible untouched." The starting point for the design was the exposed concrete block walls and the concrete floors. "It consists of raw and modern elements placed in careful relation to one another." The store is white, bright and light!

The in-fill is a detached drywall ceiling with recessed lighting, prefabricated display units, cash wrap counter and floating sand-blasted glass panels.

The simplicity of the design and the neutral colors of the setting creates a gallery like setting for the product which is displayed like artwork. The shoes are paraded along the glass shelves that are cantilevered off of the plinth-like partitions that stand out in front of the natural, concrete block walls. The smart and contemporary furniture not only provides seating but creates a sophisticated residential setting which is further enhanced by the rose colored shag rug on the cool concrete floor. "A sense of tranquility fills the interior and makes the product the main focus."

Blitstein says, "The final result is a pure architectural space with a very strong statement about the type of simple but elegant interior design being expressed."

DUNE

DESIGN: **Skakel & Skakel,** Edinburgh, Scotland
FIXTURES/FITTINGS: **Vitrashop**

THOUGH DUNE is an established chain of shoe stores, when the company felt a new look was needed they called upon Skakel & Skakel, of Edinburgh, to redesign and revitalize the firm's retail image. This meant not only new retail store designs but company graphics, packaging and point-of-sale material. The designers were asked to keep the store fluid and flexible so that the space could easily be reconfigured by the staff as the merchandise changed and "to keep the element of surprise for the regular customer."

According to Simon Hardwick, Dune's retail operations director, "the fashion footwear market is one where image is important. The new design has significantly enhanced our brand communication process, giving us a clear and consistent identity. The homogenous look makes customers feel very much at home, whether they're in the new shop in Glasgow or a re-branded store on King's Road in London."

The new design calls for warm maple veneers, limestone slab floors and pale yellow plaster work walls which are complemented with cool washes of blue from concealed lighting "to reflect the Dune brand palette." All of the light, modular and moveable floor and wall fixtures/fittings, were created and produced by Vitrashop for the Dune company.

Wall panels of frosted glass are accented with stainless steel pegs and brackets and they tie in with the arced, triple shelf floor units. These wood based, arced segments support the frosted glass shelves of the same contour design by means of brushed stainless legs. Depending upon the spacial requirements, the arcs can be reconfigured into new shapes and profiles. Arcs and curves are repeated on the walls as well as in the sweep of the centrally located cash/wrap desk.

This store was honored with the prestigious Scottish Design Award for retail interior design.

ROCKPORT

Newbury St., Boston, MA

ARCHITECT & DESIGN: **Bergmeyer Associates,** Boston
PRINCIPAL IN CHARGE: **Joseph P. Nevin, Jr.**
PROJECT DESIGNERS: **Laura Regrut, IIDA & David J. Mayer, RA**
SR. PROJECT MANAGER: **Ross Sinclair Cann, AIA**
PROJECT LEADER: **Joseph J. Zelloe, AIA**
JOB CAPTAIN: **John V. Weglarz**
ASST. DESIGNERS: **Karla Fernandes / Timothy R. Fink /
Kelly McDonald / Maria Panagopoulou**
PROJECT TEAM: **Christopher F. Dolan**

ROCKPORT PROJECT TEAM
SVP, GLOBAL BRAND MARKETING: **Linda Lewi**
DIR. OF RETAIL: **Nick Palihnich**
DIR. OF CREATIVE DEVELOPMENT: **Jonathan L. Lander, ISP**
VISUAL MERCHANDISING: **Nicole Gamst / Kristin Lauer**
ART DIRECTION: **Scott Cirlin**

PHOTOGRAPHY: **Lucy Chen Photography,** Somerville, MA.

THE BACK BAY BOSTON flagship for Rockport was designed by the Boston based architecture and design firm, Bergmeyer Associates. Rockport's new concept of "New Comfort" was to permeate the total environment. The concept was evolved to address the emotional as well as physical aspects of comfort. According to Rockport, "When you're comfortable you can do anything." Bergmeyer's challenge was to infuse the store with "a sense of calm energy and carry the qualities of lightness and engineered comfort found in the product into the new prototype."

Throughout the space is light, open and inviting. Warm white paint with a sheen cover the walls and the glass and wood display systems, though they appear light and floating, are sturdy. The physical space is long, narrow and bi-level. The entrance level is connected to the rear selling space by a flight of six

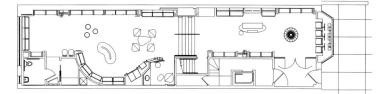

steps. The "Comfort Zone" serves as the transition between the women's and men's areas: the men's area is up front and the women's products are at the rear of the mezzanine. The "Comfort Zone" supports the basic concept that "footcare is not only essential to good health, but a healthy state of mind-and a healthy state of mind enables one to relax and find balance in an otherwise chaotic environment." To stimulate the senses, the designers used a variety of textures and surface treatments. Located within this "zone" are foot massages and reflexology treatments, citrus based footcare products and custom foot beds can be fitted. The circular rotunda in the ceiling, over the zone, glows with a blue/green light that catches the shopper's eye and brings him/her up the steps. The elliptical cash/wrap counter is located at ground level in the men's area. Here the floor is paved with gray slate tiles.

The light natural wood and pale cream space is accented with the "colors of nature": green, blue and purple. These colors appear on the custom settee and as accent colors on some focal walls.. The blue/green glow of the rotunda also recalls these colors as do the color stripes on the beige carpet on the upper level. The pull-out stools are also upholstered in these colors. There are streamlined, state-of-the-art fluorescent fixtures mounted on the thin shelves to light up the shoes and bags being displayed Highlighting both areas are backlit frosted panels-inspired by the frenell lens found in lighthouses. Indirect lighting within the soffit of the ceiling softens the edge and "enforces the quality of glowing light" found throughout the store.

HUSH PUPPIES

Parque Arauco, Santiago, Chile

DESIGN: **FSL & Associates,** Santiago, Chile
Francisco Saavedra Larrain & Marcela Ponce de Leon S.
V.M. DESIGNER: **Bernardita Oyarzun D.**

SINCE THE HUSH PUPPIES' store in the Parque Arauco Mall in Santiago is the flagship store for the shoe chain in Chile, it was selected to be redesigned in readiness for the new century. FSL & Associates, Architects of Santiago, were selected to affect the new look.

According to Francisco Saavedra Larrain, who designed this store along with Marcela Ponce de Leon S., "The new architectonic proposal tries to give the client a maximum of fluid movement inside a neutral setting—casual, elegant, almost without any ornament but with very good illumination." The space is divided into several areas: women, men, children, outdoor, sportswear, casual and accessories. A new area, Client Service, was also added where the shopper can relax, read, watch TV, have some coffee while deciding on a purchase. Each area is easily identified.

The diagonal glass storefront is accented by white niches in the curved wall on the interior that flows back to the main

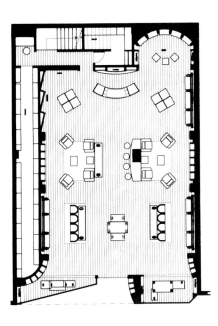

body of the store. More niches appear, outside, to the right of the entrance into the store. A white marquee with black lettering overhangs the doorway. Inside, the perimeter walls are white and they support "the floating exhibition elements:" display units made up of light wood uprights with glass shelves and metal trim. These are used to display the featured shoes in the different areas. The maneo wood that is used for the wall and floor fixtures contrasts with the cherry wood flooring.

Seating is provided throughout but it varies with the area. Upholstered armchairs appear in the more "elegant" or "dress" areas while benches are provided for the children. Carpets are laid out beneath the seating.

Display tables are used to add to the residential quality of the space and they complement the seating arrangements.

The tables are constructed of the same light wood that is used on the wall piers and capped with glass shelves. The cash/wrap also serves as a display area for accessories and the familiar "dog" on the counter—the Hush Puppies logo basset hound—becomes a friendly focal point up front. Throughout, the lighting is most important and in addition to the wall washing luminaries and dicroic lights in the niches of the curved wall, there are also aluro metal lamps in the ceiling as well as focusable spots targeted at the shoes on the glass shelves.

REDWING SHOE CO.

Mall of America, Bloomington, MN

DESIGN: **SteinDesign,** Minneapolis, MN.
DESIGN DIRECTOR: **Sanford Stein**
PROJ. DESIGNER/ENVIRONMENTAL GRAPHICS: **Andy Weaverling**
PROJ. DESIGNER/ARCHITECTURAL INTERIORS: **Joel Woodward**
CAD MNGR.: **Jim Hoepfl**

Redwing Shoe Co. Team
PROJECT MANAGER: **Arne Skyberg**
DESIGN COORDINATOR: **Nick Farsted**

THE REDWING SHOE COMPANY has a 100-year heritage but it is mainly noted for the construction boots and shoes it produces. In addition, the company has three other lines: Irish Setter—an outdoor, recreational line; Vasque—a climbing, trail and back-packing shoe line; Worx—a moderately priced, more stylish work shoe collection.

SteinDesign was challenged to create a branded environment that would exemplify the strategic positioning and values of the four brands and place them in their proper settings. "Taking the cue from the firm's history." The brick store front is reminiscent of a local cobbler's shop in the 1920s. The "Interpretive Center," located at the front of the store, not only establishes

an emotional connection with the customer but increases their awareness of
the Red Wing brand roots. It takes
them on a virtual tour of the manufacturing process through museum-like
displays, vintage photos and interactive
videos.

In each of the four brand areas
strong brand graphics are merged with
artifacts. A construction site highlights
the Red Wing brand. The area is complete with a full scale crane and peep-
holes that provide videos of construction site activity. The rear end of a util-
ity vehicle and gravel on the floor serve
to set off the Worx brand. Shoppers
can "flex and feel" the Vasque brand in
a waterfall / circulating pool setting
with a range of floor surface to try out
the shoes on. Irish Setter is comfort-

ably set on a back porch of a rustic, natural wood vignette of an "up north" cabin. The POS station appears as a lodge and it serves to anchor the outdoor recreational brands of Vasque and Irish Setter. Customers are encouraged to test the footwear in the theme appropriate settings which seem to float from one to the next. "Throughout the store, the use of honest, industrial materials create authenticity and reinforce the brand's positioning as essential equipment to get the job done."

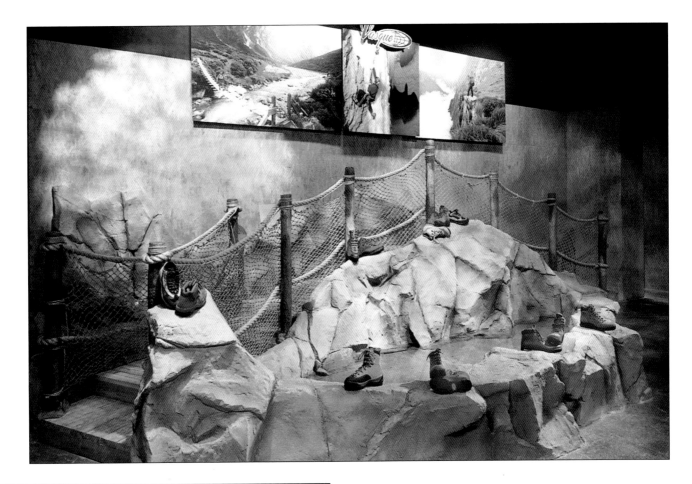

TIMBERLAND

The Parisian, Birmingham, AL

DESIGN: **Fitch,** Worthington, OH

RECENTLY unveiled in the Parisian Department Store in Birmingham, AL is the new vendor shop concept created by Fitch of Worthington, OH for the Timberland Company. Timberland manufactures premium quality footwear, apparel and accessories and the company's goal was to "create a powerful and consistent retail presence across all of its channels including department stores, independent retailers and sports speciality stores." The designs, shown here, serve as a foundation for Timberland's brand presentation including branded shop-in-shop environment, and a modular point of purchase system.

The challenge was to translate Timberland's brand values of rugged durability, quality and integrity into fixtures, systems, displayers and signage. The resultant design program includes fixtures and furniture made of warm,

matte wood and all signs and banners reinforce the famous Timberland logo and tree design. All of the merchandised materials are crafted from the signature orange leather that is used in lining the Timberland icon product—the yellow boot— and includes the signature four rows of white stitching along the seam lines. The color palette throughout continues with the use of natural earth tones.

The new P.O.P. system is a flexible modular kit of fixtures and displayers. The system can be assembled from a basic starting point with elements added as needed. Included in the system is a shadowbox element which introduces consumers to Timberland's community service

ethics and activities as well as a free-standing "waterfall" which conveys the company's outdoors heritage. Also included is a 3D table top display which features Timberland's icons: the signature orange leather signs with tree logo and white stitching.

"With the new flexible system,

Fitch devised a solution that powerfully reinforces Timberland's brand yet represents both a cost effective and timely solution for a major national program," said Christian Davies, Fitch's V.P. and project manager for this design challenge.

FOSSIL

Universal CityWalk, Orlando, FL

DESIGN: **JGA Inc.,** Southfeld, MI
DESIGN TEAM
CREATIVE DIRECTOR: **Mike Curtis**
PROJECT MANAGER: **Vicki Gilberston**
SR. DRAFTSPERSON: **Curt Nemith**
PROJECT SERV. DIRECTOR: **Ernie Szczerba**
ASST. PROJECT DIRECTOR: **Jeremy Grech**
COLORS & MATERIALS: **Stephanie Gach**

CLIENT'S DESIGN TEAM
EXEC. VP: **Richard Gundy**
VP STORES: **Tom Olt**
DIR. OF VM/STORE DESIGN: **Jody Clarke**
PROJECT MANAGER/STORE DESIGN: **Rita Randolph**

ARCHITECT OF RECORD: **Cuhaci & Peterson**, Orlando, FL
PHOTOGRAPHY: **Laszlo Regos Photography**, Berkeley, MI

HOW TO SHOW and arrange micro scaled merchandise such as watches and sunglasses in a macro space of 30' x 40' with a 40' ceiling? That was the problem that JGA Inc. of Southfield, MI had to solve in designing the new Fossil store on Universal's CityWalk in Orlando, FL. In addition, the space had to "create a thematic and entertaining experience that captures the hip, nostalgic essence of the Fossil brand and complements the excitement of the CityWalk."

The Fossil store is located on a corner that offers the entertainment center visitor a first exposure to the theme park beyond. Two "attention-grabbing," over-sized rocketship shaped signs with chasing lights are used for identification and they take their design cue from the pylon signs of the Sputnik era. Large poster frames—like those used in movie houses—are also framed with chasing lights

and they highlight some of the products "now showing" inside the store. The store's interior celebrates the 1950s and the floor plan is accented with vertical elements that draw the shoppers through the space. Adding to the 50's flavor of the design concept is the canopied fixture that recalls a Service Station of the period, a "drive-in "movie screen at the rear of the store that shows a montage of vintage TV shows and classic ads. Nostalgic icons from Fossil's archives of "brand art" reinforce the brand name and also enhance the space.

"Fossil offers a fresh vantage point of streamline moderne, marrying nostalgic references with contemporary style and finishes." Though the sun may be shining brightly outside, the ceiling of the store is painted midnight blue to create a nighttime ambience. The fixture towers seem to disappear into the dark ceiling and the graphics, around the perimeter, are high-

lighted by lights from suspended tracks. Old fashioned street lamps add to the overall ambience. At the center of the store is the watch showcase and canopy with the oversized illuminated letters that spell out "Fossil"—like at a 1950s gas station. Sunglasses are displayed under the "drive-in" movie screen at the rear of the store and signature, '50s style gas pumps help to recall "the good old days."

The fixtures are a mixture of honey-toned and cherry stained maple with rounded corners. To restate the streamline moderne influence, stainless steel bands trim the interior soffit and the exterior showcase windows. They also serve as linear accent striping. The concrete floor, stained a rust color, is accented with painted Fossil logos . To highlight the merchandise in this night-time setting, recessed canopy lights and suspended track lights are used throughout the space.

EuroConcept
Shopfitting, Store Equipment,
Lighting Technology,
Refrigeration Equipment,
Building Technology

EuroSales
Visual Merchandising,
Sales Promotion,
POS Marketing

EuroShop

The Global
Retail Trade Fair
Düsseldorf
Germany
www.euroshop.de

Feb. 23-27, 2002

EuroCIS
Communications,
Information,
Security Technology

EuroExpo
Stand Construction,
Design, Special Events

Messe
Düsseldorf
North Amer